★ ★ ★ The Aut

Texas Ranger COOKBOOK

Published by Harris Farms Publishing
Hamilton, Texas

THE AUTHORIZED TEXAS RANGERS COOKBOOK

Courtesy of Bob Mitchell Collection

Captain Bob Mitchell, Company F, retired, Gaines de Graffenreid, Curator, Texas Ranger Museum, and Alva Stem, Retired, Director of Parks and Recreation for the City of Waco. The rifle being held is the one Davy Crockett was using when he died defending the Alamo.

DEDICATION

I dedicate this book to my good friend Gaines deGraffenreid, long time curator of the Texas Ranger Museum and Hall of Fame. He was largely responsible for its development into what it is today. Also to my old friend Ranger Bill Gunn who introduced me to my wife, Cheryl. And lastly, to Captain Bob Mitchell and Captain James Wright who have been good friends through the years.

First Printing	10,000	October, 1994
Second Printing	10,000	May, 1995
Third Printing	5,000	June 1996
Fourth Printing	5,000	February 2005

Published in the United States of America
Harris Farms Publishing
P.O. Box 191, Hamilton, Texas 76531
254-386-5103

LCCN: 94-079713
ISBN: 0-9641614-0-0

cookbook resources®

541 Doubletree Drive
Highland Village, Texas 75067
(972) 317-0245

Manufactured in China

THE RANGERS PRAYER

O God, whose end is justice
Whose strength is all our stay
Be near and bless my mission
As I go forth today.
Let wisdom guide my actions,
Let courage fill my heart
And help, Lord, in every hour
to do a Ranger's part
Protect when danger threatens,
Sustain when trails are rough;
Help me to keep my standard high
And smile at each rebuff.
When night comes down upon me,
I pray thee, Lord, be nigh,
Whether on lonely scout or camped,
Under the Texas sky.
Keep me, O God, in life
And when my days shall end,
forgive my sins and take me in,
for Jesus' sake, Amen.

Written by Pierre Bernard Hill
Chaplin Texas Rangers
Contributed by Lewis C. Rigler, Retired
and wife Joyce

About The Authors...

I've always been interested in cooking. I watched my mother cook and was fascinated by it when I was a small child. She cooked lots of cakes and pies for all occasions and everyone in the family had to have an angel food cake on his or her birthday. Mother finally wrote a cookbook which was well received and sold out two editions. We plan to bring out a third edition of it soon. It had a lot of our family recipes in it which had been handed down through the years. My folks on both sides of the family were good cooks and mother had all their recipes plus a lot she'd gotten from good friends through the years.

When my wife Cheryl and I got married I had no idea she could cook and I really didn't care, because I knew I could. When she began to unpack her things, she had a large collection of recipes and cookbooks and practically the same kitchen utensils I had. I was amazed to find that besides being so charming and pretty she could cook.

For many years I've been a pecan grower and have an especially large collection of pecan recipes. One of my favorites was a recipe that we got from LBJ's cook when he was President. It's the best pecan pie recipe I've ever found. When I would have company and want to show off, I'd always make an LBJ Pecan Pie. Cheryl found my recipe and made it one day. Hers was so much better than mine that I've never made one since.

Cheryl and I were down at the Texas Ranger Museum one day visiting with our friend, Tom Burks. Tom asked me what I was doing since I had suffered a heart failure and had to slow down. I told him that we were going to put together a couple of cookbooks to give me something to keep me occupied for a while. I asked him what ever happened to the cookbook someone was going to put together for the Rangers back several years ago. He said that no one ever went through with it, but if we wanted to work on it he would give us the files he still had.

We started with these old files and then wrote to the Rangers, both active and retired, asking them to send us recipes and stories. The response has been good and we hope that what we've come up with will be interesting and informative.

The Texas Rangers are a great organization and without them the history of Texas would be a lot different than it is today. The Rangers have served the people of Texas well for 171 years and I hope they will continue to serve them for at least another 171.

Cheryl Harris   Johnny Harris

Photograph courtesy of Capt. Bob Mitchell

Old Time Rangers on scout

TEXAS RANGERS

The Texas Rangers were born in 1823 when Stephen F. Austin, known as the Father of Texas, hired 10 men to protect his colony and paid them out of his own pocket. Texas Rangers from 1823 on have protected Texans and their property from Indians, Mexicans, bandits and any other enemy. Before being hired a Ranger had to answer three questions: Can you ride? Can you shoot? Can you cook? These were the elements required to make him self-sufficient. Rangers had to learn to ride like a Mexican, trail like an Indian, shoot like a Tennessean and fight like the devil. Indian Chief Quanah Parker, the last great Comanche Chief, said "Rangers don't fight like white people."

The rebel Texas government approved the original organization of a corps of gunmen in 1835. This corps was called "Texas Rangers". It set up three companies, each to be headed by a Captain with First and Second Lieutenants. A Major was the overall head of the organization. The Captains and Major were elected by popular vote of the delegates. Privates were enlisted for one year at $1.25 per day. Each Ranger had to furnish his own horse, saddle, bridle, gun and one hundred rounds of ammunition. The Ranger carried only the bare necessities; a blanket, a little buckskin leather pouch for salt, parched corn and tobacco, a canteen, rope and ammunition. Of course, all carried a rifle, pistol and knife. Other than these essential items, they had to live off the land. Sometimes this created a problem. The old timers said before the Rangers came, the Indians carried off their children, and after the Rangers came, something carried off their pigs and chickens.

Until the 1840's the Indians had a real advantage over the men with guns. An Indian could get off a lot of arrows from a horse while a man with a gun was on the ground re-loading. When a reliable repeating pistol was developed the Rangers learned to shoot from horseback at full speed.

The old time Rangers had to have a lot of sheer guts to do the things they did. They nearly always fought under adverse circumstances when severely outnumbered. They had to be without fear to fight under the conditions that usually existed. So great was their reputation that Sam Houston said, "You could withdraw every regular soldier from the border of Texas, if you would give her but a single regiment of Texas Rangers." There was no other organization like the Rangers whether it be Army or local law enforcement organizations. The Rangers always stepped in to handle situations that others couldn't. They were always there whether it be military insurrections, corruption in local law enforcement departments, gangsters, union problems or whatever; they were all taken in stride.

In 1918 national prohibition was passed. The 18th Amendment caused a serious problem for Texas. Texas has 1,248 miles of common border with Mexico. This has created problems for many years and a lot of the time it has fallen the duty of the Texas Rangers to patrol these long stretches, mostly along the Rio Grande. Many times they counted the weeks on end, living off the land. Smugglers began bringing in illegal booze from Mexico as soon as prohibition was passed. They were known as "tequileros" and came across the Rio Grande every night. It was brought across on pack mules and later transferred to a more modern means of transportation.

By the 1920's when Ranger's went on a scout they carried a pack mule with flour, beans, coffee, hog jowl, potatoes, syrup, sugar and dried fruit. A scout is what any reconnaissance mission was called, whether they were in pursuit of bootleggers, outlaws or gathering information for any reason.

For many years the Rangers were under the direct control of the Governor and the Adjutant General. This was quite a problem at times because of political influence and corruption. After Governor Jim Ferguson was impeached he ran his wife, Miriam (Maw) Ferguson for Governor. Governor Ross Sterling was her opponent and was supported by all the Rangers. When she was elected over thirty Rangers resigned. The day she was inaugurated two Rangers escorted her to the podium. The day she took office she fired all of the Rangers, including her escorts, and appointed her own friends. She made over 2,000 appointments, among them many known criminals, bootleggers, gamblers and ex-convicts.

In 1935 when governor James Alred was elected on a Reform Platform he got the Legislature to pass a bill creating the Department of Public Safety. From this time forward the Highway Patrol and the Rangers have come under one department.

Photograph courtesy of Capt. Bob Mitchell

"1936" Modern-day Texas Rangers

The Texas Rangers were the models for many other states' agencies such as Arizona, Oregon, New Mexico, Nevada, Colorado, California and others. This organization is older and more prestigious than any other on the North American continent, including the Royal Canadian Mounted Police which was established in 1873.

I can not imagine Texas without Texas Rangers. In my lifetime I've seen so many times when the Rangers had to be called in due to corruption in various law enforcement agencies, riots and union problems. Surely the people of Texas and our politicians will continue to recognize the need and necessity of having such a fine and distinguished organization as this in perpetuity.

ACKNOWLEDGEMENTS

The Texas Rangers share a long, rich and colorful history with Texas and Texas Tradition. It is our hope that you will enjoy reading about the proud heritage of the Texas Rangers through some of their own culinary contributions and the early history of the organization.

Enjoy the vintage photographs taken from the extensive collection of Texas Ranger Captain Bob Mitchell, Texas Ranger Bill Gunn and the Texas State Library via John Anderson.

Study the wonderful and historically correct drawings of old guns and equipment that would have been used on the trail, by award-winning Texas Artist W. L. "Bill" Chappell.

Special thanks to ALL Texas Rangers, both active and retired, and their families, as well as the Texas Ranger Association Foundation Members and their families, who contributed tried and true "family favorite" recipes and interesting stories for everyone to enjoy. Many thanks to everyone who has worked on this book, just to name a few...Constance and Herman Price—computers, Ann Price, Wendy Peel, Sugar Gunn, Renae Gromatzky, Allyson Poteet, Cathy Brumbalow—office manager and Brandi Loftis—office-runner.

We gratefully acknowledge Tom Burks—Curator, Texas Ranger Museum, for all of his help in general from start to finish. A contribution is made to the Texas Ranger Museum and Hall of Fame for each book sold. Thank you Sheryn Jones and Josie Ware for your expertise and organization skills, Wimmer Co., Inc. Cover art by Bob Hayton.

Within the pages of this first cookbook ever written for the Texas Rangers, we hope they find pride, spirit, and strong leadership evident in the history of their organization, that has held true from the very beginning until today. Spirit, pride and leadership that we hope will continue forever for the benefit of the State of Texas and the people who live there.

Johnny and Cheryl Harris with artist Bill and Faye Chappell

TABLE OF CONTENTS

Texas Rangers and River Guards
Lower Rio Grande Valley

Nibblin's

SAMUEL H. WALKER

Photograph courtesy of Archives Division - Texas State Library

Samuel H. Walker

Samuel H. Walker's name is indelibly stamped on the history of Texas and the Rangers. He was born in Maryland in 1810. Before coming to Texas he had fought in the Indian Wars in the southeast. Sometime after 1836 he came to Texas and joined Captain Jack Hays' company in San Antonio. Walker was sent by Hays to Patterson, New York to help Samuel Colt redesign his pistol so it would be practical for use by the Rangers. The result was the gun known as the 'Walker Colt'. Colt's original pistol was light weight and had to be taken apart to reload. It was impossible for a man traveling at high speed on a horse to reload since the gun had to be taken apart in three pieces. Walker and Colt became good friends and in about a month Walker returned to Texas with a new pistol. The grip fit the hand better and the trigger was changed and a trigger guard was used instead of a folding trigger. The cylinder was lengthened so that a heavier bullet could be used. A lever rammer was put under the barrel to seat the bullet in the chamber so the cylinder would not have to come out for reloading.

The Mexican War began in 1846. Captain Jack Hays was made Colonel of a Texas Ranger company which was a part of the U. S. Army. All the old Rangers had 'Walker Colts' and everyone that joined the company wanted one of these superior pistols. Hays sent Walker to New York to find Colt and get him to make a thousand pistols; two for each Ranger. Colt had gone bankrupt in 1842, but kept his patents. He designed another gun known as 'The Old Army' and got the Whitney Gin Co. to manufacture the guns for him. These guns got to Colonel Hays' men soon after they landed in Vera Cruz, Mexico.

Samuel Walker held a commission as Captain of the Mounted Rifles in the regular U. S. Army, however, he was still looked upon as a Texas Ranger. He never changed his tactics from those of a Ranger Captain and for this reason he met an untimely end on October 9, 1847. He died leading a charge against Santa Anna, hoping to capture the Mexican General. After the Mexican forces retreated, Walker lay dead with a bullet through his head and another through his chest. His men burst into tears when they saw him. It was said that there was never a braver or more faithful officer than Captain Samuel H. Walker.

JOHN COFFEE "CAPTAIN JACK" HAYS

Photograph courtesy of Archives Division - Texas State Library

John Coffee (Captain Jack) Hays

John Coffee "Captain Jack" Hays came to Texas in 1837. He was 21 years old, and a surveyor by trade. He was a very well liked young man and developed into an excellent Indian fighter. Hays joined the Rangers in 1838 and by the age of 23 was made a Captain in charge of protecting San Antonio, Texas. The different Mexican factions always wanted to capture San Antonio. The city also had to be constantly guarded since the Indians still raided from time to time.

Captain Jack joined a band of friendly Delaware Indians in 1838 to study their war tactics. He was a natural fighter and leader and although he was short and slight of build, he was recognized as a fearless fighter. A band of Indians had been stealing horses and raiding homesteaders around San Antonio. Hays and a group of Rangers tracked them to the mouth of the Uvalde Canyon where they were located by a flock of buzzards. Buzzards always followed the Indian camps because of their habit of killing fresh meat. There were 12 Indians and all but 2 were killed. The stolen horses were returned to San Antonio to their owners. Hays later organized a force of 50 men and 10 Lipan Indians led by Chief Flacco to pursue Indians that were raiding and terrorizing settlers in the Llano and Fredericksburg area. This scouting expedition later became known as the "Battle of Llano".

Hays, being a surveyor, always was interested in the layout of the country around him. He climbed up on Enchanted Rock to look around while everyone had stopped to rest. He found more than one hundred Indians on the other side and they charged him. He fired every shot he had and took out his Bowie knife and was ready to defend himself to the very last when his friends finally came to his assistance after having heard the shots.

Hays and Chief Flacco came upon about one hundred Comanches. During the fight that followed Hay's horse ran away and carried him through the Indian lines. Chief Flacco, thinking that he was charging, followed him. When the Captain and the Chief got through they went around the flanks and got back to their men. Chief Flacco said later, "Me and Red Wing not afraid to go to Hell together. Captain Jack heap brave man, not afraid to go to Hell by himself."

When Hays left the Rangers in 1848 for California, Hays County, Texas was named for him. He went to San Francisco where he served as Sheriff for four years during the Gold Rush. He was named Surveyor General of California and laid out the City of Oakland, becoming it's first resident. He was a delegate to the 1876 Democratic convention from California. He came back to Texas on visits, but remained in California the rest of his life where he died in 1883.

SPINACH DIP

- 1 (10 ounce) package chopped frozen spinach
- 1 box Knorr vegetable soup mix
- 1½ cups sour cream
- 1 cup mayonnaise
- 1 can chopped water chestnuts
- 3-4 chopped green onions

Thaw spinach and squeeze dry. Mix all ingredients. Cover and chill for about 2 hours. Hollow out a small bread loaf to serve dip in, or you may just serve it with vegetables, crackers or chips.

Captain Bruce M. Casteel, Headquarters Company

Bill Gunn, Retired, and wife Sugar

A Ranger Captain was down on the Rio Grande with his company of men tracking bandits. They had the gang of bandits spotted and were about to engage them in battle when the Captain asked his men to kneel in prayer before the battle. He said, "Lord, if you'll just stick around for a few minutes you'll see the golldangdest fight you ever witnessed. And Lord, if you can't see fit to help us, just please don't help them."

Bill Gunn, Retired

CRAB DIP

- 6 ounces drained, flaked crabmeat
- 8 ounces cream cheese
- ¼ cup mayonnaise
- 3-4 tablespoons milk
- ¼ teaspoon snipped chives
- ⅛ teaspoon garlic powder
- 6 ounces hot pepper sauce
- dash salt
- snipped chives

Remove cartilage from crabmeat. In a small mixer bowl beat together cream cheese, mayonnaise, milk, ¼ teaspoon chives, garlic powder, pepper sauce and salt. Stir in crabmeat; chill thoroughly. Garnish with additional snipped chives. Serve with assorted raw vegetables.

Sergeant Kyle Dean, Company B

MUSHROOM & BACON DIP

- 10 slices bacon
- 1 pound thinly sliced mushrooms
- 1 cup thinly sliced onion
- 2 cloves minced garlic
- 1 envelope Lipton Secret Recipe onion soup mix
- ⅛ teaspoon black pepper
- 8 ounces softened cream cheese
- ½ pint sour cream

Cook bacon in medium skillet. Remove and crumble. Reserve 2½ tablespoons drippings. Add mushrooms, onion and garlic to reserved drippings and cook over medium heat for 5 minutes or until mushrooms are tender and liquid is almost evaporated. Stir occasionally. Add onion soup mix and pepper, then cream cheese. Combine thoroughly. Simmer, stirring constantly, until cream cheese is melted. Stir in sour cream and bacon, heat through. Garnish, if desired, with parsley, additional mushrooms or bacon. Serve with assorted breads and crackers. Yield: 2 cups of dip.

Bill Gunn, Retired, and wife Sugar

ARTICHOKE DIP

- 1 cup grated Parmesan cheese
- 1 (14 ounce) can artichoke hearts, well drained and chopped
- 1 cup salad dressing
- 1 cup chopped green chilies
- 2-3 chopped green onions with top
- 1 clove garlic

Stir together ingredients in a shallow microwave safe bowl and heat until bubbly; stir. If preparing in conventional oven preheat oven to 350° and bake for 20 to 25 minutes.

John Barron Harris, Texas Ranger Association Foundation, and wife Cheryl

BARBECUED PECANS

- 2 tablespoons apple cider vinegar
- 1 tablespoon honey
- 4 cups pecan halves
- 1 tablespoon butter
- seasoned salt

Combine vinegar and honey. Mix well. Fill 2 pint jars with pecan halves. Divide the honey and vinegar mixture evenly and pour over pecan halves. Shake well and rotate until all pecans are coated. Pour pecans in shallow pan and broil at 250° for 10 minutes, stirring often. Remove from oven. Add butter and seasoned salt to taste. Put back in oven for 10 to 15 minutes. Remove and cool. Store in refrigerator.

Glenn Krueger, and wife Jackie

SOUTHERN COATED PECANS

- 1 cup sugar
- ½ cup cold water
- ¾ teaspoon salt
- 1 teaspoon vanilla
- 1 teaspoon cinnamon
- 1 pound pecan halves

Combine sugar, water, salt, vanilla and cinnamon. Cook 10 minutes or until bubbles cook down. Add pecans and stir until all pecans are coated. Continue stirring until syrup turns to sugar. Pour onto cookie sheet and separate.

Glenn Krueger, and wife Jackie

SAUSAGE BALLS

1 pound hot sausage
8 ounces grated mild longhorn cheese
2 cups biscuit mix

Combine all ingredients and mix well. Form into small balls the size of quarters. Place on ungreased cookie sheet. Bake at 350° for 20 minutes. To keep hot, place on hot dish with toothpicks placed in them. Can be served with a mild dip or with a drink. This is very good.

Sergeant Jim Gillespie, Company C

Glenn Krueger, and wife Jackie

ZIPPY CHEESE ROLLS

8 ounces cream cheese
1 pound American cheese
1 pound sharp Cheddar cheese
1 pound pasteurized process cheese spread
1 tablespoon garlic powder
12 minced jalapeño peppers
8 ounces chili powder

Soften cream cheese to room temperature; all other cheeses cold. Grate all cheese, except cream cheese. Mix thoroughly all cheeses, garlic powder and jalapeños. Knead well and mold into long rolls (whatever size you want). Roll in chili powder until well covered. Wrap in wax paper. Chill thoroughly before slicing.

Selwyn H. Denson, Retired, and wife Lois

This recipe has become a tradition in our family for years during the Christmas season. We make them together because there is some work to it. The recipe can be doubled or even more if necessary, depending on how many you want to make.

BITZI'S CHEESE BALLS

- 6 ounces blue cheese
- 2 (5 ounce) jars processed Cheddar cheese spread
- 4 (3 ounce) package cream cheese
- 1 teaspoon Worcestershire sauce
- 2 tablespoons grated onion
- ½ teaspoon Accent
- 1 cup ground pecans (optional)
- ⅓ cup parsley flakes

Have cheeses at room temperature. Mix all cheeses, Worcestershire, onions and Accent until thoroughly blended. Add half of the pecans and half of the parsley. Put in foil paper and shape. Cover and refrigerate over night. About one hour before serving, roll ball in the remaining pecans and decorate with the remaining parsley. Do not put in the freezer. Will keep in refrigerator indefinitely.

John Barron Harris,
Texas Ranger
Association Foundation,
and wife Cheryl

For best results always use the very finest ingredients.

CHEESE BALL WITH CURRY

- 1 (8 ounce) package cream cheese, softened
- 1 pound jalapeño Velveeta cheese spread
- ½ cup chopped pimiento-stuffed olives
- curry powder
- ½ cup chopped pecans

Combine the cheeses and olives in a bowl using a fork or your hands. Mix in curry powder to taste. Form into rolls. Refrigerate. Before serving, roll in pecans until entirely covered. Serve with crackers. Do not use processor—must be mixed by hand.

John Barron Harris,
Texas Ranger
Association Foundation,
and wife Cheryl

PARTY PECAN CHEESE BALL

- 1 (8 ounce) package cream cheese, softened
- 1 cup shredded extra-sharp Cheddar cheese
- 1½ teaspoons Worcestershire sauce
- ¼ teaspoon salt
- ¼ teaspoon onion powder
- 1 (2 ounce) package blue cheese, crumbled
- ½ teaspoon red pepper
- ¼ teaspoon garlic powder
- ½ cup finely chopped pecans

Combine all ingredients except ¼ cup pecans. Mix well. Shape into a ball, and coat with remaining pecans. Yield: 1 cheese ball.

John Barron Harris, Texas Ranger Association Foundation, and wife Cheryl

OLIVE CHEESE BALL

- 2 (8 ounce) packages cream cheese, softened
- 1 envelope Italian salad dressing mix
- 2 teaspoons olive juice
- ¼ teaspoon cayenne pepper
- 4 cups shredded mild Cheddar cheese
- ¼ cup chopped pimiento-stuffed olives
- ¼ teaspoon garlic salt
- 1 cup chopped pecans

Combine all ingredients except pecans. Mix well. Shape into a ball. Roll in pecans. Yield: 1 cheese ball.

John Barron Harris, Texas Ranger Association Foundation, and wife Cheryl

FRIED JALAPEÑOS

1 (14 ounce) can whole jalapeño peppers
½ cup finely grated longhorn cheese
2 eggs
½ cup milk
flour

Cut caps off jalapeños, or leave stems intact and make a slit down the sides of peppers. Carefully remove seeds and membrane without tearing the peppers. Stuff each jalapeño with about ½ teaspoon of cheese, pressing it into pepper with your little finger. Mix eggs and milk. Roll pepper in flour, then in egg mixture and again in flour. Set aside to allow the coating to set while you heat oil to 350°. Deep-fry peppers until they are browned (no more than 1 minute). Do not serve to cowards or Yankees. Yield: 6 or more servings.

Bill Gunn, Retired, and wife Sugar

STUFFED GREEN CHILIES

1 (8 ounce) can whole green chilies
1 cup grated sharp Cheddar cheese
6 beaten eggs
¼ cup milk
1 tablespoon mustard
1 pound cooked, crumbled sausage

Carefully slit chilies lengthwise, wash, remove seeds. Drain on paper towels. Spoon 1 to 2 tablespoons cheese in each chili. Arrange spoke fashion in a lightly greased pie pan. Combine eggs, milk, mustard and sausage. Pour over chilies. Bake at 350° for 15 minutes. Add rest of cheese, bake an additional 5 minutes or until set. Yield: 6 servings.

Bill Gunn, Retired, and wife Sugar

STUFFED BANANA PEPPERS

- 20 banana peppers
- 1 (7 ounce) can Albacore tuna, in water
- 1 egg, boiled and mashed
- 2 tablespoons minced onion
- 1/4 cup sweet relish
- 1/3 cup mayonnaise
- 1 teaspoon prepared mustard
- 1/2 teaspoon seasoned salt
- 1/2 teaspoon black pepper
- 1/4 cup chopped pecans

Slice peppers in half lengthwise and take the seeds out. Combine remaining ingredients and mix well. Fill pepper halves and refrigerate until ready to serve.

John Barron Harris, Texas Ranger Association Foundation, and wife Cheryl

LAURA'S TORTILLA ROLL-UPS

- 2 (3 ounce) packages cream cheese
- 1/2 cup finely chopped black olives
- 1/2 cup finely chopped green olives
- 1 cup finely chopped pecans
- 1/2 cup finely chopped celery
- 3-4 chopped jalapeño peppers
- 1 package flour tortillas

Mix all ingredients and spread on tortilla. Roll up and hold in place with toothpick. Slice into rounds and serve. May be served with picante sauce.

Capt. James Wright, Retired, and wife Laura

FRIED OYSTERS

Place oysters in bowl of buttermilk. Remove oysters separately and roll in mixture of half cornmeal and half cracker meal. Salt and pepper to taste. Cook oysters in peanut oil in deep-fryer. Cook at temperature you would fry fish. Oysters will brown quickly. Another way to cook is soak oysters in beer and then lightly roll in flour. Cook the same way. Do not overcook!

Max Womack, Retired

DATE DELIGHTS

- 8 ounces chopped dates
- 2 cans sweetened condensed milk
- 2 cups chopped nuts
- Ritz crackers
- 1 box confectioner's sugar
- 2 sticks margarine
- 8 ounces cream cheese
- 1 teaspoon vanilla

Cook dates and milk until thick. Be careful - it scorches easily. Add nuts and spread on crackers. Bake 8 minutes at 350°. Cool. Cream together confectioner's sugar, margarine, cream cheese and vanilla. Spread on top. Yield: 50 to 60.

Lloyd Johnson, Retired

TEXAS CAVIAR

- 1 package dry Italian dressing mix
- 1 tablespoon vinegar
- 2 cans black-eyed peas, rinsed and drained
- 1 large bell pepper, diced
- 1 bunch green onions, chopped
- ½ teaspoon garlic powder
- ½ cup chopped jalapeño peppers

Mix Italian dressing according to package directions, adding vinegar. Combine dressing with remaining ingredients and refrigerate. Serve with crackers.

Sergeant Jim Gillespie, Company C

Red or green bell peppers may be used. A small jar of diced pimientos may be substituted for the bell pepper.

SUMMER SAUSAGE

- 2 pounds ground beef
- 1½ teaspoons Liquid Smoke
- 2 tablespoons Morton's Tender Quick
- 2 tablespoons peppercorns
- ¼ teaspoon garlic salt
- ¼ teaspoon onion salt
- 1 cup water

Mix all ingredients together. Divide into 3 rolls. Wrap in plastic wrap and refrigerate for 24 hours. Bake uncovered on wire rack at 300° for 1 hour and 15 minutes.

Sergeant Jim Gillespie, Company C

PICKLED EGGS

- 1 cup pickled beet juice
- 1 cup vinegar
- 4 cups water
- 1 clove garlic
- 1 medium bay leaf
- 2 teaspoons mixed pickling spices
- ½ teaspoon salt
- 1 small sliced onion
- 12 hard-cooked eggs, peeled

In a large bowl combine beet juice, vinegar, water, garlic, bay leaf, pickling spices and salt. Mix well. Separate onion into rings. Add onion and eggs to vinegar mixture. Cover and refrigerate for several days.

Gaines de Graffenried,
Late Curator
Texas Ranger Museum
and Hall of Fame

Submitted by his son, Tommy de Graffenried.

VEGETABLE BARS

- 2 tubes refrigerated crescent rolls
- ¾ cup mayonnaise
- ½ cup sour cream
- 8 ounces softened cream cheese
- 1 package ranch dressing mix
- ¾ cup chopped green pepper
- ¾ cup chopped green onions
- ¾ cup diced tomatoes
- ¾ cup chopped broccoli
- ¾ cup diced carrots
- ¾ cup diced cauliflower
- ¾ cup grated cheese

Cover bottom of 11x17-inch baking pan with crescent rolls, patting the rolls to fit the pan. Bake at 350° for 7 to 8 minutes or until lightly browned. In bowl, combine mayonnaise, sour cream, cream cheese and dressing mix. Spread evenly over cooled crust in pan. Combine all vegetables and grated cheese. Spread over cream cheese mixture, pushing the vegetables in slightly. Cover with plastic wrap and refrigerate 3 to 4 hours. Cut in bars and serve. Half a recipe can be prepared in a 9x13-inch pan.

Sergeant W. R. "Bill" Gerth,
Company C,
and wife Dixie

Photograph courtesy of Bill Gunn Collection

Group of old time Rangers — on the far right is Capt. John Hughes in his younger days.

Dough-Si-Dough

Early day wolf hunt with President Theodore Roosevelt in Oklahoma in which he was accompanied by Ranger Captain Bill McDonald.

ROBERT McALPIN WILLIAMSON

Photograph courtesy of Archives Division - Texas State Library

Robert McAlpin Williamsom

Robert McAlpin Williamson was born in Georgia in 1804. When he was 15 he was confined to his home because of an illness that left him crippled for life. This ended his formal schooling but did not slow him down on getting his education. He studied law while he was in bed and passed the Georgia Bar before he was 19. He carried on an active life determined not to let his handicap bother him.

His right leg was pulled back at the knee. The wooden leg that he wore from his knee to the ground resulted in him being called "Three Legged Willie". He was quite a ladies man, played the banjo and danced better than most men.

Williamson came to Texas in 1826. He was a very effective politician and judge in the early days of the Republic of Texas. He moved to San Felipe de Austin where in 1829 he and a partner started a paper called "The Cotton Plant". He was a very prolific writer and immediately incurred the wrath of the Mexican government with the editorials he wrote about Texas gaining it's independence. He became known as the "Patrick Henry of the Texas Revolution".

He was sent to Mina to the consultation and the rebel government commissioned him Major on November 29, 1835 and ordered him to organize a corps of Rangers. He was in William Smith's cavalry company in the Battle of San Jacinto. On December 26, 1836 the first Congress of the Republic of Texas elected him judge of the Third Judicial District. This automatically made him a member of the Supreme Court. In 1840 he was elected to represent Washington County in Congress. He served in the fifth, sixth and seventh Congress. He also served in the eighth Senate and in the House again in the ninth. After annexation he served in the Senate of the first and second Legislature, retiring in March, 1848.

He was a great orator, politician, judge, writer and legendary figure of the Texas Revolution. After being defeated in the 1849 race for Congress he returned to his farm near Independence, Texas. He and his wife Mary Jane raised seven children. In 1857 an illness left him incapacitated. He died at the home of his father-in-law in Wharton, Texas on December 22, 1859. Williamson County, created in 1848, was named for him.

BEN McCULLOCH

Photograph courtesy of Archives Division - Texas State Library

General Ben McCulloch

Ben McCulloch was born in Tennessee on November 11, 1811. He was a neighbor of Davy Crockett and was coming to Texas with him except that Crockett left early after a political defeat. Crockett died in the Alamo, and had McCulloch arrived in Texas with him he also would have been at the Alamo. McCulloch got to Texas a few days after Crockett and in time to be in command of artillery at San Jacinto.

Although he never had a chance to have formal schooling he became well educated by reading everything he could find. After the War for Independence McCulloch settled in Gonzalez where he was a surveyor. He was elected to Congress in 1839. During this time he still led an active military life fighting Indians and Mexicans.

During the Mexican War in April 1846 General Zachary Taylor asked the Texas Governor for four regiments of Texas Rangers to be mustered into the U. S. Army to act as scouts and to advise him of the best route of attack against the Mexican Army. One of the companies was led by Ben McCulloch and it fell his responsibility to look over the territory between Fort Brown and the Mexican Army in Monterrey, Mexico. He had an uncanny ability to penetrate the enemy lines and return safely with information as to their whereabouts and troop strength.

McCulloch went to California in 1849 where he served as Sheriff of Sacramento County from 1850 to 1852. In 1853 he was commissioned U. S. Marshall and in 1857 appointed to a peace commission to help settle Mormon trouble in the Utah Territory. When Texas seceded from the Union McCulloch was commissioned a Brigadier General in the Confederate Army and assigned to protect the Indian Territory west of Arkansas and south of Kansas. He went inside the enemy lines alone on the second day of the Battle of Elkhorn to learn the position and strength of the enemy. He was killed by a sharpshooter on March 7, 1862, and is buried in the state cemetery at Austin.

McCulloch is remembered as a great Texas patriot and McCulloch County was named for him when it was created in 1856.

BATTLE OF PLUM CREEK

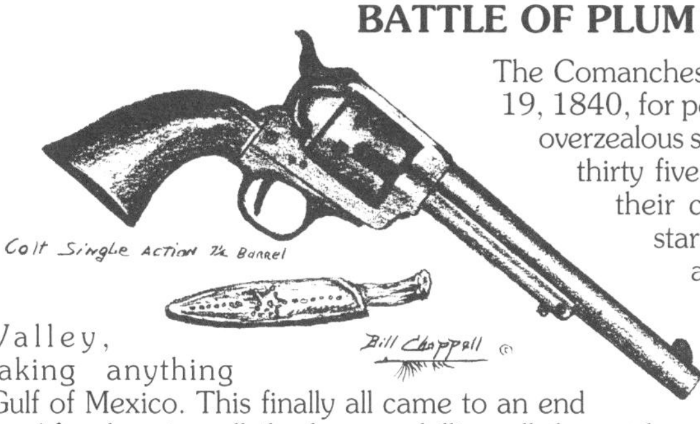

The Comanches met in San Antonio on March 19, 1840, for peace talks. During the talks some overzealous soldiers started shooting and killed thirty five Comanches, including most of their chiefs. The council house fight started the war with the Comanches and they took revenge by going down the Guadalupe River Valley, burning white settlements and taking anything they wanted, all the way to the Gulf of Mexico. This finally all came to an end south of Victoria at Linville.

After burning all the houses, killing all the cattle and taking everything they wanted they started the long trip back home. This was a slow process since they had nearly three thousand horses and mules plus all their plunder. McCulloch's Rangers caught up with them on August 11, 1840, at Plum Creek near the town of Lockhart. The Rangers had the new Colt pistols which fired five shots before having to be reloaded.

The Rangers quickly defeated the Comanches and this ended one of the worst Indian wars in Texas history.

TEXAS GOVERNOR ANN W. RICHARDS' JALAPEÑO CHEESE CORNBREAD

- 1½ cups cornbread mix
- ¾ cup milk
- 1 egg
- ½ cup green onion, chopped
- ½ cup creamed corn
- ¼ cup chopped jalapeño pepper
- ¾ cup grated cheese (Cheddar, Monterey Jack or both)
- 1 tablespoon sugar
- 2 tablespoons oil
- bacon bits, chopped pimiento, garlic to taste

Combine all ingredients and mix well. Pour into buttered baking dish and bake at 425° for about 25 minutes or until done. This is a wonderful recipe. It is particularly good with chicken or pork and any vegetable.

Texas Governor
Ann W. Richards

GRANDMA WRIGHT'S BREAD

- **2 packages yeast**
- **2 teaspoons salt**
- **⅔ cup sugar**
- **½ cup melted shortening**
- **½ cup hot water**
- **3½ cups warm water**
- **10 cups flour (approximate measure)**

Put yeast in a bread bowl, add salt. Add sugar, shortening and water (Better water be too warm than too cold). Mix. Add flour until it gets thick. Turn onto bread board. Knead until waxy or stiff. Put in bowl, let rise in a warm place until doubled (about 1½ hours). Put on board and work some more. Cut in four parts, put in greased loaf pans, let rise until doubled. Bake 30 minutes to 1 hour in 275° to 350° oven. Yield: 4 loaves.

Capt. James Wright, Retired, and wife Laura

In the 1970's and 1980's my widowed mother, Estella, baked bread once a week, usually a double batch. Neighbors, friends and children would put in orders or just drop by hoping to be lucky enough to get a loaf of her bread.

BOOTLEGGER BREAD

- **1 can beer**
- **3¼ cups flour**
- **¼ teaspoon salt**
- **3 tablespoons sugar**
- **3 teaspoons baking powder**
- **2 tablespoons melted butter**

Mix all ingredients until a sticky dough is formed. Allow to rise in a greased, covered bowl for 1 hour. Pour into greased loaf pan. Smooth top of dough. Bake at 350° for 1 hour. Brush with melted butter last 10 minutes of baking. Yield: 1 loaf.

Sergeant L. R. "Rocky" Wardlow, Headquarters Company

Substitute 2 cups of self-rising flour for flour and baking powder above. Bake in 5x9-inch loaf pan 35 to 40 minutes. Metal pan bake at 375°, glass pan bake at 350°.

During a company meeting near Giddings, Texas, this became a favorite of Sheriff Joe Goodson of Lee County. In fact, Sheriff Goodson called my wife specifically to get this recipe.

QUICK YEAST BREAD

- 2 packages yeast
- 1 cup lukewarm water
- 1 teaspoon sugar
- 1 cup scalded milk
- 2½ teaspoons salt
- 6 tablespoons sugar
- 2 beaten eggs
- 6-7 cups flour
- 6 tablespoons melted shortening

Soften yeast in lukewarm water (I have learned this must be somewhere between 105° and 115° for yeast to work) with 1 teaspoon sugar. Scald milk (I do this by adding boiling water to powdered milk) stir in the salt and sugar. Cool until lukewarm. When cool, stir in yeast mixture; then beaten eggs. Add about 4 cups of flour and beat until smooth. Add cooled, melted shortening and beat smooth. Stir in rest of flour using just enough to make dough almost too stiff to beat with a wooden spoon. Beat until smooth. Cover the bowl and let rise in a warm place about 1 hour until just double in bulk. Turn out onto lightly floured surface, and shape into rolls or 3 small loaves. Place in greased pans, cover and let rise again in a warm place until double in bulk - about 45 minutes. Bake rolls 15 to 20 minutes at 400°. Bake loaves 20 minutes at 400°, then reduce heat to 350° and bake 20 minutes longer.

Captain Carl Weathers,
Company C,
and wife Mickey

This recipe is from my mother, Estelle Weathers.

CAMP BREAD

- 2 cups flour
- 2 teaspoons baking powder
- 1 teaspoon salt
- 2 tablespoons oil
- 1 cup milk

Mix dry ingredients. Add oil and milk. Roll out 3/4-inch thick like biscuit dough. Preheat covered skillet for 5 minutes on medium low heat. Put in dough and spread out to cover bottom of 10- or 12-inch skillet. Cover and bake 6 or 7 minutes. Turn and bake 5 more minutes.

Toliver H. Dawson, Retired

GREEK BREAD

- 1 loaf French bread
- 1/2 cup mayonnaise
- 1/2 cup softened margarine
- 2 cups shredded mozzarella cheese
- 6 chopped green onions
- 1 small can chopped black olives
- 1/2 teaspoon garlic powder

Split bread lengthwise and cut in half. Combine all other ingredients and mix well. Spread on bread. Bake at 350° for 15 minutes.

Sergeant Kyle Dean, Company B

DROP BISCUITS

- 2 cups flour
- 3 tablespoons baking powder
- 1/2 teaspoon salt
- 3 1/2 tablespoons shortening
- 1 cup milk

Combine dry ingredients; cut in shortening. Add milk, mix well. Drop onto cookie sheet and bake 15 minutes at 425°.

Sergeant Jim Gillespie, Company C

PARKER HOUSE ROLLS

⅔ cup dry powdered milk
2 cups boiling water
½ cup shortening
⅓ cup sugar
2 packages yeast
2 tablespoons sugar
⅓ cup warm water
3-4 cups flour
¼ cup water
½ teaspoon soda
1 teaspoon baking powder
1 teaspoon salt
5 cups flour

Put powdered milk, boiling water, shortening, and ⅓ cup sugar in a large mixing bowl to dissolve sugar and shortening. Dissolve yeast with 2 tablespoons sugar and ⅓ cup warm water (105° to 115°). Set aside. Add 3 to 4 cups of flour to milk mixture, one cup at a time, mixing with mixer after each cup. Add yeast mixture. Mixture should be the consistency of cake batter. Set in warm place to rise for about 2 hours. Keep a watch so batter does not spill out of bowl. When it starts to do that, stir back down. After 2 hours add ¼ cup water with baking soda, baking powder and salt dissolved in it. This mixture will bubble. On clean surface spread out 3 cups flour. Pour dough mixture onto flour and top with 2 cups flour. Work with hands until flour is all worked into dough. Mold in rolls or bread loaves, put into greased pan. Brush with melted margarine and cover. Let rise, then bake in 350° oven - rolls 20 to 30 minutes, loaves 40 to 45 minutes.

Captain Carl Weathers,
Company C,
and wife Mickey

This recipe is from my mother, Estelle Weathers.

COMPANY'S COMING BISCUITS

- 6 cups all-purpose flour
- ½ cup sugar
- 1 tablespoon salt
- ½ cup shortening
- 2 packages yeast
- 1 cup lukewarm water
- 2 cups buttermilk

Combine flour, sugar and salt. Cut in shortening until well mixed. Dissolve yeast in water and add to flour mixture. Add buttermilk and mix well. Pinch them off, roll in flour and work with hands into rolls. Place on ungreased cookie sheet or in greased muffin tins. Let rest 30 minutes in warm place and bake at 375° until brown. I keep this dough stored in a zip-lock bag in my refrigerator all the time. They are great for unexpected but welcome guests! Will keep 2 to 3 weeks in refrigerator.

John Barron Harris,
Texas Ranger
Association Foundation,
and wife Cheryl

RANCH STYLE BISCUITS

- 1 package yeast
- ½ cup warm water
- 2 tablespoons sugar
- 2 tablespoons baking powder
- ½ teaspoon soda
- 4 tablespoons shortening, melted
- 1 teaspoon salt
- 2 cups buttermilk
- 5½-6 cups flour

Dissolve yeast in warm water. Mix all ingredients together. Knead lightly. Refrigerate or bake immediately. Bake at 450°. Yield: 34 biscuits

Cathy Brumbalow
Office Manager
Harris Farms

Substitute whole wheat flour for ½ the flour measure.

DUTCH OVEN BISCUITS

- **2 cups flour**
- **¼ teaspoon salt**
- **3 teaspoons baking powder**
- **2 heaping tablespoons shortening**
- **milk**

Mix together dry ingredients. Cut in shortening. Add in milk. Use whole or skimmed sweet milk or canned evaporated milk mixed with 2 parts water or ½ milk and ½ water. Mix; enough to make dough so it can be put on floured board, then roll and cut biscuits. Usually the biscuit will be lighter if dough is not worked too much. Place in greased pan and cook till golden brown.

John Barron Harris,
Texas Ranger
Association Foundation,
and wife Cheryl

I usually make these in a Dutch oven. Place 3 small rocks in the bottom of the Dutch oven. Set the Dutch oven on a bed of coals. Grease a tin pie pan and fill with biscuits and place the pie pan on top of the 3 rocks, then cover with lid and shovel live coals around sides and on top of Dutch oven. By using this method you can cook several pans of biscuits in the same Dutch oven. When I was 16 years old I began helping cook for a group of hunters out in the Davis Mountains. The man doing the cooking was an old friend of mine, Marcus Gist, and this was the recipe that we used. We would mix them up dry the night before and before daylight we'd get up and mix in the milk. This was many years before Bisquick or any of the mixes were ever introduced to the market. If he'd have only realized what he had in this mix he could have come out with ready mix long before it was developed.

BUTTER HORNS

- 1 cup scalded milk
- ½ cup shortening
- ½ cup sugar
- 1 teaspoon salt
- 1 cake yeast
- 3 beaten eggs
- 4½ cups flour

Combine milk, shortening, sugar and salt. Cool to lukewarm. Add yeast and stir well. Add eggs, then flour. Mix until a smooth, soft dough. Knead lightly on floured surface. Place dough in greased bowl, cover and let rise till double in size. Divide dough into thirds. Roll each third on lightly floured surface into a 9-inch circle. Cut each circle into 12 to 16 wedges. Roll each wedge starting with wide edge. Arrange on greased baking sheet and brush with melted fat or salad oil. Cover and let rise until very light. Bake at 350° until done, 8 to 10 minutes.

Sergeant Gary Henderson,
Company F,
and wife Sally

NAVAJO FRY BREAD

- 3 cups flour
- 1½ teaspoons baking powder
- ½ teaspoon salt
- 1⅓ cups warm water

Mix flour, baking powder and salt. Add warm water and mix. Dough should be soft but not sticky. Knead until smooth. Tear off a chunk about the size of a peach. Pat and stretch until it is thin. Poke a hole through the middle and drop into sizzling hot, deep fat. Lard is traditional but you can use vegetable oil. Brown on both sides. Drain and serve hot with honey or jam. Yield: 4 to 6 servings.

John Barron Harris,
Texas Ranger
Association Foundation,
and wife Cheryl

Substitute 1½ cups white and 1½ cups of whole wheat for flour.

HOT WATER CORNBREAD

1 cup cornmeal
1 tablespoon salt
boiling water

Mix cornmeal and salt. Add water to form a moist dough - not too wet. Shape into patties. Flatten (about palm size) and then fry until golden brown in hot grease turning once. Drain and serve with fresh butter.

Sergeant Matt Cawthon,
Company F

This is a late 1800's to early 1900's recipe from my maternal grandmother, Mary Polk. We still enjoy it today.

MEXICAN CORNBREAD

1 cup cornmeal
1 cup milk
½ teaspoon salt
½ teaspoon soda
2 beaten eggs
1 can cream style corn
1 can Ranch Style beans
½ cup bacon drippings
¾ pound ground beef
1 large chopped onion
½ pound grated cheese
2 chopped jalapeño peppers

Mix together cornmeal, milk, salt, soda, eggs, corn, beans and bacon drippings. Pour ½ of batter into greased casserole dish. Brown the meat, drain. Layer the meat, onion, cheese and peppers. Cover with remaining batter. Bake 40 to 45 minutes at 350°.

Glenn Krueger, and wife Jackie

TEXICAN CORNBREAD

1 pound ground beef
1 cup self-rising cornmeal
½ cup oil
1 cup buttermilk
2 well-beaten eggs
1 pound cream style corn
½ pound grated Cheddar cheese
1 large onion, chopped
½ chopped bell pepper

Grease large skillet or casserole and place in 350° oven. Brown the meat. Mix cornmeal, oil, buttermilk and eggs. Add corn, mix well. Pour half of the cornbread mixture in heated skillet. Sprinkle on cheese, then layer onion, pepper and meat. Cover with remaining cornbread mixture. Bake 45 minutes or until golden brown.

**Captain Bruce M. Casteel,
Headquarters Company**

JALAPEÑO CORNBREAD

½ pound bacon
3 cups cornbread mix
1½ cups milk
½ cup oil
1 large jar diced pimientos
1 tablespoon minced garlic
1 can cream style corn
3 beaten eggs
1½ cups grated cheese
2 tablespoons sugar
1 large onion, chopped
chopped jalapeño peppers to taste

Fry bacon crisp; drain and crumble. Mix all ingredients well. Bake in greased pan in preheated oven at 425° for 40 to 45 minutes, or until center is done.

**Bill Gunn, Retired,
and wife Sugar**

PERFECT CORNBREAD

- 1 cup sifted all-purpose flour
- ⅓ cup sugar
- 4 teaspoons baking powder
- ¾ teaspoon salt
- 1 cup yellow cornmeal
- 2 eggs, beaten
- 1 cup milk
- ¼ cup shortening

Sift flour with sugar, baking powder and salt. Stir in cornmeal. Add eggs, milk and shortening. Mix with a wire whisk or spoon until just blended. Do not overbeat. Spoon into greased cast iron cornbread pan (these come in various shapes and sizes - stick, pie shape, muffin, etc.). Bake at 425° for 20 minutes or until browned. Cornbread won't usually stick if you first grease the pan and heat in the oven until very hot, then spoon in batter.

Cheryl Harris,
Texas Ranger
Association Foundation

I have used this recipe for years with great success. Never fails!

FRIED CORN BREAD

- 1 cup cornmeal
- 1½ teaspoon baking powder
- ¾ cup milk
- 1 cup shredded Cheddar cheese
- ⅔ cup flour
- ½ teaspoon salt
- ¼ cup melted margarine
- 1 egg, beaten

Combine dry ingredients, add combined milk, margarine and egg, mixing just until moistened. Stir in cheese. For each serving, spoon approximately ¼ cup of mixture onto a hot, lightly greased griddle or skillet and flatten slightly. Cook until lightly brown on both sides. If batter becomes to thick, add a small amount of milk.

Sgt. Billy Peterson, Company C
and wife Barbara

CHILI CORNBREAD

- 1 package cornbread mix
- ½ cup sour cream
- 2 tablespoons chopped bell pepper
- 1 tablespoon chopped green onion
- 2 teaspoons chili powder
- ½ cup softened butter or margarine
- ¾ teaspoon chili powder

Make cornbread according to package directions, adding sour cream, pepper, onion and 2 teaspoon chili powder. Cook as directed on package. Mix butter and ¾ teaspoon chili powder to serve with hot cornbread. You may use muffin tins to bake bread in.

Glenn Krueger, and wife Jackie

Either red or green bell pepper may be used.

LIGHT CORNBREAD

2½ cups cornmeal cooked in 1½ quarts (6 cups) of boiling, salted water for 20 minutes over low heat. When mush is cool, add 1 yeast cake that has been dissolved in ¼ cup water. Let sit over night. The next morning, add ½ cup syrup, ⅓ cup oil or margarine, and 6 to 7 cups of flour. Let rise till double in size. Make into loaves and let rise. Bake at 375° for 45 to 50 minutes.

**John Barron Harris,
Texas Ranger
Association Foundation,
and wife Cheryl**

This recipe belonged to my Grandmother Harris and great grandmother Sample and was given to me by my Aunts Mary Frances Robert and Winnie Brown, Brazos County, Texas.

CORN DODGERS

- 1 cup stone ground cornmeal
- 1 cup flour
- 4 teaspoons baking powder
- 1 teaspoon salt
- 1 egg
- ¼ cup oil
- 2 tablespoons sugar

Mix all ingredients. Add enough milk to make a batter like you are making pancakes. Heat oil in an iron skillet. Pour the batter into round corn dodgers. Turn the dodgers over until golden brown on both sides.

**Sergeant John Aycock,
Company F,
and wife Estelle**

LEVI DUNCAN CORNBREAD

- 1 pound lean ground beef
- 1 cup sifted flour
- ¼ cup sugar
- 4 teaspoons baking powder
- ¾ teaspoon salt
- 1 cup cornmeal
- 2 eggs
- 1 cup milk
- ¼ cup softened shortening
- 1 (#2) can drained whole kernel corn

Brown meat, drain excess fat. While meat is browning sift together flour, sugar, baking powder and salt. Stir in cornmeal. Add eggs, milk and shortening. Stir until mixture is smooth and lumps dissolved. Do not overbeat. Spread browned ground meat in bottom of a large iron skillet. Spread drained whole kernel corn over meat. Spoon in cornbread mixture. Flavor with finely chopped jalapeño peppers if desired. Bake at 425° for 20 to 30 minutes or until a golden brown. If cooked outdoors in Dutch oven, allow 5 to 10 minutes more.

Edgar D. Gooding, Retired

One slab of this and a bowl of pintos will carry you all day.

A friend of mine owned a very large ranch in the Hill Country of Central Texas. At the ranch headquarters was a cook shack referred to as the "Chuck Wagon". The cook was a man of large stature and a bushy shock of white hair. His disposition was that of a rattler that had just been rousted from his den. Not now and then, but every day. None of the ranch hands fooled with him; just respect.

During shearing time the ranch owner had a set up to shear the sheep and goats on the east side of the ranch and then move to the west side. For convenience (and I believe a bit of nostalgia) the ranch owner let the old cook pull his chuck wagon to the different spots and cook outdoors for the ranch hands and the shearing crew. This was a full blown chuck wagon the old man had fixed to suit his needs and desires. All seasonings and mixins were handy. The tail gate let down to make a table to work and serve from. When it let down there were two legs that dropped in place to hold it.

There was a young man from Austin who was a 'wannabe' cowboy. He couldn't go to the horse trap and bring in the saddle horses without his red neckerchief, leather wrist cuffs, leggins (chaps), spurs and the works. His father owned a smaller ranch where this young man worked for awhile with me and my Father. But he wanted bigger and better so he went to the larger ranch. He and the old cook crossed.

They were set up on the east side shearing area and had a picket line for the horses about 50 yards from the chuck wagon. When the older hands came in for lunch they tied their horses at the picket and walked to the wagon for dinner. The young man came in at a full gallop, slid his mount to a halt and made a flying dismount. The old cook told him to get that blankedy-blank horse out of my camp.

The next day the same thing happened. The young man came flying into camp, slid to a halt in a cloud of dust, made his fancy dismount, tied the reins to the wagon wheel and started for the coffee pot. The old cook said nothing, but walked over in front of the horse, took off his flour coated apron and flapped it about twice in the horse's face. Well sir, the wreck was on the way. The horse reared back against the reins, turning the wagon wheel about a quarter turn and moving the wagon forward. The legs under the tail gate collapsed and down came the table with dinner, spices and all into the dirt. The old cook walked over to the fire and picked up his fire stick (a hard, well-seasoned oak limb used to poke the fire). He went after the young man whippin' him between the shoulders with the burned end of the stick leaving a black mark with each lick.

Needless to say, the young man was very unpopular with the other hands that day. Working all day with no lunch or coffee and riding so close to the man responsible must have been a fine example of self control for them. Either that or they figured he had been punished enough for his misdeed.

Edgar D. Gooding, Retired

HUSHPUPPIES

1¾ cups water
1 cup cornmeal
1 tablespoon flour
¼ teaspoon salt
¾ teaspoon baking powder
¼ cup chopped onion
¼ teaspoon black pepper

Beat all ingredients together until thoroughly mixed and slightly thick. Drop batter from tablespoon onto hot, well-greased griddle. Flavor can be enhanced by depressing center of dough and adding any leftover meats, fish or vegetables. When brown on one side, flip and brown on other side.

Sergeant Jim Gillespie,
Company C

PIZZA CRUST

1 package yeast
1 cup warm water
1½ cups flour
1 teaspoon sugar
1 teaspoon salt
1 tablespoon shortening

Dissolve yeast in warm water. Mix well. Add flour, sugar, salt and shortening; mix. Add more flour until dough is firm. Knead. Press in pizza pan or 9x13-inch pan. Spread tomato sauce over crust and layer on any or all of the following: parsley flakes, sliced olives, mushrooms, picante sauce, chopped onions, sliced jalapeños, thin sliced sausage, mozzarella cheese, hoop cheese, thin sliced pepperoni or browned, drained hamburger meat. Bake at 375° to 400° until brown.

Glenn Krueger, and wife Jackie

PUMPKIN BREAD

- 3½ cups flour
- 3 cups sugar
- 1½ teaspoons salt
- 2 teaspoons soda
- 2 teaspoons cinnamon
- 4 eggs
- 1 cup oil
- 1 cup pecans
- 1 cup raisins
- ⅔ cup water
- 2 cups pumpkin

Combine all ingredients. Mix well by hand. Pour in well-greased and floured coffee cans. Fill cans exactly ½ full or they will run over. Bake for 1 hour at 350°. Wrap in foil after removing from can. Yield: 4 - 1 pound coffee can cakes.

Bill Gunn, Retired, and wife Sugar

This recipe is one of my mother's favorites. She was the first female Deputy Sheriff of Bell County, Texas. Mrs. Ivy Mae Gunn, 1905 to 1986.

MADELYNE EASON'S BANANA-PECAN BREAD

- 6 bananas
- 2 cups sugar
- 1 cup margarine
- 4 eggs
- 4 cups flour
- 2 teaspoons soda
- 1 teaspoon salt
- 1 cup pecans
- 1½ teaspoons vanilla

Mash bananas with a fork. Combine all ingredients. Mix by hand - no mixer. Pour into a well greased and floured pan. Bake at 325° for 1 hour. Do the toothpick test. Makes enough for neighbors!

John Barron Harris, Texas Ranger Association Foundation, and wife Cheryl

Use bananas after they have turned brown on the outside. Makes the bread more moist.

STRAWBERRY BREAD

- 3 cups flour
- 1 teaspoon salt
- 2¼ cups sugar
- 1¼ teaspoons baking soda
- 1 tablespoon cinnamon
- 4 eggs, beaten
- 1¼ cups oil
- 2 cups chopped pecans
- 1 (16 ounce) package frozen strawberries; thawed and drained; retain juice
- 2 cups confectioner's sugar
- 1 tablespoon lemon zest
- 4 tablespoons lemon juice
- red food coloring

Combine flour, salt, sugar, baking soda and cinnamon. Make a well in the center and add eggs and oil. Mix thoroughly. Add pecans and strawberries and strawberry juice. Pour into greased and floured loaf pans. Bake at 350° for 40 minutes for small loaves, or 60 minutes for large loaves. For glaze, mix sugar, lemon zest and lemon juice. Add enough food coloring for strawberry pink. Yield: 6 small loaves or 2 large loaves.

**John Barron Harris,
Texas Ranger
Association Foundation,
and wife Cheryl**

BANANA BREAD

- 1¾ cups flour
- ⅔ cup sugar
- 1 tablespoon baking powder
- ½ tablespoon salt
- 2 eggs, slightly beaten
- ¼ tablespoon baking soda
- ½ cup shortening
- 1 cup mashed bananas
- 1 cup pecans

Preheat oven to 350°. Grease and flour 9x5-inch loaf pan. In a large bowl, with fork, mix first 5 ingredients. With pastry blender or 2 knives used in scissors-fashion, cut in shortening until mixture resembles coarse crumbs. With fork, stir in bananas and eggs just until blended. Spread batter evenly in pan. Bake 55 minutes to 1 hour until toothpick inserted in center comes out clean. Cool in pan on wire rack 10 minutes. Remove from pan and cool completely on rack. Makes one loaf.

**Lt. Earl R. Pearson, Company F
and wife Patricia**

OUT OF THIS WORLD PECAN WAFFLES

- 2½ cups flour
- 4 teaspoons baking powder
- 1½ tablespoons sugar
- ¾ teaspoon salt
- ¾ cup oil
- 2¼ cups milk
- 2 eggs, beaten
- ½ cup ground pecans

Measure and sift dry ingredients together. Mix oil with milk and eggs. Stir into dry ingredients. Mix until smooth. Add pecans and mix well. Bake immediately or let set in the refrigerator over night. They will keep well covered for 2 weeks. Easy and good.

John Barron Harris, Texas Ranger Association Foundation, and wife Cheryl

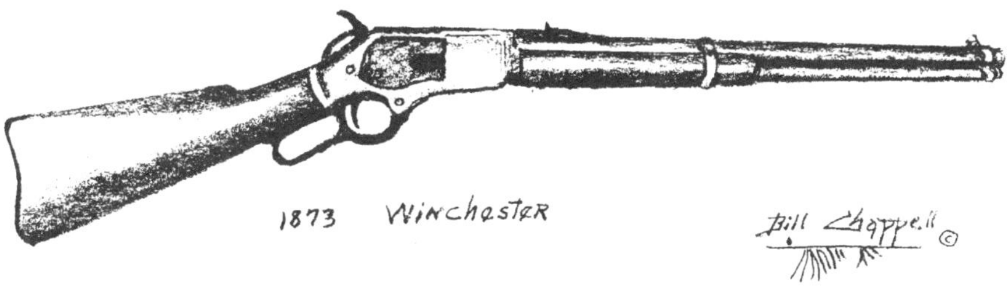

1873 WINCHESTER
The rifle that won the West!

Man in center of picture is General W. W. Sterling, the only man to hold every grade in the Texas Ranger Service all the way to Adjutant General of Texas.

★ ★ ★ ★

Ranger Treats

Captain D. W. Roberts' Ranger Camp, below Ft. McKavett, Texas, in Menard county, 1878. Photo made by M. C. Ragsdale.

CAPTAIN JOHN SALMON "RIP" FORD

Photograph courtesy of Archive Division - Texas State Library

John Salmon "Rip" Ford

Captain John Salmon "Rip" Ford was a man of many talents. He was a doctor, surgeon, lawyer, surveyor, writer, politician and one of the toughest fighters of the Mexican War. As an officer under Colonel Jack Hays' command, as well as doctor and surgeon, it fell his duty to notify all next of kin of casualties. Being a writer he would end his letters with 'Rest in Peace'. There were so many men killed in battle that he began to end them with 'R.I.P.' From this time on he was known as "Rip" Ford.

When Hardin Runnels was elected Governor in 1858 there was more fighting and bloodshed than at any time since the Texas Revolution in 1836. Governor Runnels was determined to stop the bloodshed. He commissioned Ranger Rip Ford to Supreme Commander of all state forces. His orders were to stop the Indian problems, even if he had to go across the Red River into Indian territory. This, of course, was in violation of federal law. Ford sent his first report from Brown County, Texas, where many settlers had already moved out because of Indian raids and lack of security. He asked the Governor for twenty five more men and the Governor approved his request. Ford was told to expedite everything as soon as possible because of public opinion. Ford reached the Texas Indian reservation in March and was able to talk the reserve Indians into accompanying him since they were going against their old arch-enemies, the Comanches. In doing this he picked up warriors as well as scouts to locate the camps of the Comanches. This made it possible for him to always know their strength and location. These Indians were under the direct command of Captain S. P. Ross, son of an Indian agent. The Comanches were located, and in April Ford moved his command out. In early May Ford crossed the Red River into enemy territory. The Indians had been hunting buffalo and were easy to trail. The attack came early in the morning on May 12. Several lodges were destroyed and the Comanches left at full speed. This led the Rangers to another camp whose the Chief was "Iron Jacket". He was called this because of old Spanish armor that he wore. The Chief's armor had been fine against arrows and spears, but it wouldn't hold against rifle bullets so he was killed in the battle. When the smoke cleared seventy six Indians had been killed, three hundred horses recovered, and eighteen prisoners taken. The Rangers lost two men and two were wounded. Ford proved that the Comanches could be followed and held responsible for the depredations of the settlers.

Captain Ford also fought in what was known as the "Cortinas War" on the Mexican border. Juan N. Cortinas was a thief and murderer who amassed a large following among the Mexican people along the border. Ford was sent to south Texas by Governor Runnels after the Governor learned that Cortinas had burned and pillaged Corpus Christi. The Governor put Ford in command of all the Texas forces on the Rio Grande. Ford left Austin with only eight men and no state funds since the Treasury was empty. He picked up followers on the way down and acquired a wagon and an ambulance. They arrived on the border on December 14 during a battle that was taking place at LaEbronal. By this time Ford had fifty three men, all well armed and mounted on good horses. From this time on Cortinas' forces were put on the run, until he finally retreated to the mountains in the interior of Mexico. Colonel Robert E. Lee had been sent to command the U. S. forces along the border. He stopped the Rangers from going into Mexico in pursuit of Cortinas. It was said that Colonel Lee was such a stately soldier that he immediately commanded the respect of everyone who met him.

With the "Cortinas War" over much of the Rio Grande valley had been laid waste with much damage to American citizens. Cortinas went on to amass a great fortune and became a Brigadier General in the Mexican Army and later Governor of the state of Tamaulipas. He learned to write his name after becoming governor. He carried on under-cover raids along the border as long as he lived.

Ford went on to command the Texas Cavalry, Rio Grande Division, and engaged in border operations protecting Confederate and Mexican trade. He participated in the last battle of the Confederacy at Palmito Ranch in May of 1865.

In 1868 Ford moved to Brownsville to edit the Brownsville Sentinel. In 1872 he was a delegate to the Democratic Convention in Baltimore. In 1873 he served as cattle inspector in Cameron County and in 1874 as Mayor of Brownsville. He was a member of the Constitutional Convention in 1875 and served in the Texas Senate from 1876 to 1880. He served as Superintendent of the Texas School for the Deaf and spent his later years writing his memoirs and articles on Texas History. He was a charter member of the Texas Historical Society and wrote an article which appeared in its first publication. He died on November 3, 1897, in San Antonio.

LAWRENCE SULLIVAN "SUL" ROSS

Photograph courtesy of Archive Division - Texas State Library
Lawrence Sullivan "Sul" Ross

Lawrence Sullivan "Sul" Ross was born in Benton Fort, Iowa on September 27, 1838. In 1839 his family moved to Texas settling in Milam County. In 1849 the family moved to Waco. His father was the U. S. Indian agent of the Brazos Indian Reservation near Waco from 1855 to 1858. Sul Ross learned a lot from dealing with the Indians during this time. In 1856 he attended Baylor University and then went to Wesleyan University in Florence, Alabama, where he graduated in 1859.

While leading a company of his father's reservation Indians against the Comanches he was seriously wounded. Only through his Indian friends was he finally nursed back to health. In 1859 Sam Houston appointed Ross Captain of a company of Rangers to help in protecting the frontier of Texas. With about one hundred twenty men he attacked a large Comanche village on the Pease River and during the battle killed noted Indian Chief Peta Nocona. Peta Nocona was Quanah Parker's father. One of his squaws was a white woman who had been captured by the Indians at a young age. Her name was Cynthia Ann Parker and she was Quanah Parker's mother. This broke the power of the Comanches and Cynthia Ann Parker was taken back to her white relatives, but never adapted to white people's life after having lived with the Indians so long.

Ross resigned from the Rangers and did some diplomatic work for Governor Edward Clark among the Indians. Ross entered the Confederate Army as a Private, but promotions came rapidly raising him to the rank of Brigadier General. He and his Texas Brigade protected the Yazoo River Valley after the fall of Vicksburg and supported General Joseph E. Johnston in his effort to protect Georgia. After the Civil War ended Ross returned to his home in Waco where he farmed for a while before going into politics and becoming Sheriff of McClennan County. He served on the Constitutional Convention in 1875. He was elected to the Texas Senate for the Seventeenth Legislative session.

Ross was elected Governor and inaugurated January 18, 1887. He was the first Governor to occupy the new capitol building. On his retirement in 1891 Governor Ross was elected President of Texas A & M College which had been without a President for eight years. During his administration the enrollment increased, requiring an extensive building program and many other improvements. Governor Ross was one of the guiding lights that started Texas A & M on the road to becoming the great institution it is today. His interest in education was widely recognized and Sul Ross College at Alpine was named for him. He died while on a hunting trip to the Navasota River bottom on January 3, 1898, and is buried in Waco, Texas.

MOTHER'S LIFETIME RECIPE

- 2 heaping cups of patience
- 1 heartful of love
- 2 handfuls of generosity
- dash of laughter
- 1 headful of understanding

Sprinkle generously with kindness. Add plenty of faith and mix well. Spread over a period of a lifetime. And serve everybody you meet.

Glenn Krueger and Wife Jackie

PASTRY

- 2⅔ cups flour
- 2 teaspoons salt
- 1 cup shortening
- 6 tablespoons iced water

Mix flour and salt. Cut in shortening (an electric mixer does a good job). Add water and toss with fork until well blended. Turn out on floured board and knead 3 to 4 times. Roll out half of pastry to ⅛-inch thickness on a lightly floured board. Reserve other half for top crust.

Captain Jack Dean,
Company D,
and wife Janie

JAPANESE FRUIT PIE

- 1 stick melted butter
- 1 cup sugar
- 1 teaspoon vinegar
- 1 teaspoon vanilla
- 2 beaten eggs
- ½ cup raisins
- ½ cup pecans
- ½ cup coconut
- 1 unbaked pie shell

Mix all ingredients well and pour into pie shell. Bake in preheated oven at 350° for 45 to 50 minutes or until delicately brown.

Captain Bruce Casteel,
Headquarters Company

MILLION DOLLAR PIE

20 ounces crushed pineapple, drained
1 small tub frozen whipped topping
⅓ cup lemon juice
1 can sweetened condensed milk
1 cup nuts
2 baked pie shells

Mix all ingredients and pour into pie shells. Refrigerate for an hour or until firm.

Captain Bruce M. Casteel,
Headquarters Company

Substitute graham cracker crusts for pie shells.

FRENCH COCONUT PIE

3 eggs
1½ cups sugar
1 stick melted oleo
1 teaspoon vinegar
1 teaspoon vanilla
1 can angel flake coconut

Beat eggs (not much). Combine other ingredients and bake in pie shell until done - about one hour at 300° to 350°.

Edith Kidd
Texas Ranger
Association Foundation
Member

CHESS PIE

4 cups sugar
2 tablespoons flour
2 tablespoons cornmeal
8 eggs
1 cup milk
1 stick melted butter
2 teaspoons vanilla

Toss with fork, sugar, flour, cornmeal and add eggs, beating after each one. Add other ingredients and mix well. Pour into 2 9-inch pie shells. May add pecans or coconut if desired.

Edith Kidd
Texas Ranger
Association Foundation
Member

CHOCOLATE PIE

1 1/3 cups sugar
2 tablespoons flour
2 tablespoons cocoa
1 cup milk
3 egg yolks
1 teaspoon butter
1 tablespoon vanilla
1 baked pie shell
3 egg whites
6 tablespoons sugar

Mix 1 1/3 cups sugar, flour, cocoa, milk and egg yolks together in saucepan. Cook over low heat till thickened. Remove from heat. Add butter and vanilla. Pour into baked pastry shell and top with meringue made of egg whites and 6 tablespoons sugar. Brown in 325° oven.

Sergeant Morgan L. Miller,
Company D,
and wife Ann

CHOCOLATE CREAM PIE

1 1/2 cups sugar
1/2 cup cocoa
6 tablespoons flour
3 cups milk
3 beaten eggs
1 tablespoon butter
1 teaspoon vanilla
1 baked pie shell
3 egg whites
6 tablespoons sugar

Mix sugar, cocoa and flour in microwave dish. Add milk and egg beaten together. Mix well with wire whisk. Cook on high in microwave, beating with wire whisk every 2 to 3 minutes, till thick. Add butter and vanilla. Beat well till smooth, pour in pie shell. Cover with meringue made from egg whites and 6 tablespoons sugar. Brown in regular oven.

Sergeant Jimmy T. Hailey,
Company A

SHOO-FLY PIE

1 cup raisins
2 tablespoons butter
1 cup brown sugar
2 beaten egg yolks
2 beaten egg whites
1 pie shell

Cook raisins for 10 minutes or until water has cooked down. Cool. Cream butter and sugar. Add egg yolk and raisins. Fold in egg whites. Pour into pie shell. Bake in slow oven.

Sergeant Jim Gillespie,
Company C

JELLY PIES

- 3 eggs
- 1/3 cup milk
- 1 teaspoon flour
- 3/4 cup sugar
- 1/2 cup butter or margarine
- 1/2 cup plum or grape jelly
- 1/2 teaspoon double strength vanilla
- 1 pie shell

Beat together eggs and milk. Mix flour and sugar, then gradually add to egg mixture. Continue to beat. Add margarine, jelly and vanilla. Mix well. Pour into pie shell. Bake at 250° to 275° until filling is firm.

Captain Carl Weathers,
Company C,
and wife Mickey

This recipe was my Grandmother's, Stella Gaines.

PINEAPPLE PIE

- 1 teaspoon flour
- 2/3 cup sugar
- 3 eggs
- 1/3 cup light corn syrup
- 1/2 cup crushed pineapple
- 1/3 cup coconut
- 1/3 cup butter
- 1 unbaked pie shell

Mix flour with sugar. Cream eggs. Add to sugar and mix well. Add remaining ingredients and mix well. Pour into pie shell and bake at 350° until it is firm or until you can stick a knife into the pie and it comes out clean.

Captain Carl Weathers,
Company C,
and wife Mickey

This recipe was my grandmother's, Stella Gaines.

SUGAR FREE APPLE PIE

- 1 can frozen apple juice concentrate
- 4 tablespoons cornstarch
- 4 cups sliced golden apples
- 1 teaspoon apple pie spice
- 3-4 packets granulated sugar substitute
- 1 unbaked pie shell

Mix apple juice and cornstarch in saucepan over low heat until well dissolved. Stir in apples, spice and sugar substitute. Pour into unbaked pie shell and add top crust. Bake at 350° for 35 to 45 minutes.

Lloyd Johnson, Retired

May substitute 1 can of Lucky Leaf No Sugar Apples for apples.

RHODA'S APPLE PIE

- 3-7 tart apples
- 1 cup sugar
- 2 tablespoons enriched flour
- ⅛ teaspoon salt
- ½ teaspoon vanilla
- 1 teaspoon cinnamon
- ¼ teaspoon nutmeg
- 2 tablespoons butter or margarine
- 1 pie shell

Pare apples and slice. Combine sugar, flour, salt, vanilla, cinnamon, nutmeg and butter. Sprinkle half over 9-inch pastry-lined pie pan. Heap apples into pastry shell and sprinkle with remaining sugar mixture. Adjust the top crust. Cut holes in it. Brush top with milk and sprinkle with sugar. Bake at 450° for 10 minutes, then at 350° for 40 minutes.

Rhoda Willeford

If apples aren't tart enough, add 1 tablespoon lemon juice. Grated lemon peel may also be added, if desired. Serve warm or cold, and of course, with cheese.

L.B.J. PECAN PIE

- 1 cup sugar
- 1 cup corn syrup
- 1 stick butter
- ½ teaspoon salt
- 3 eggs, beaten
- 1½ teaspoons vanilla
- 2 cups pecans, chopped
- 1 unbaked 8-inch pie shell

Combine sugar, syrup, butter and salt. Cook until dissolved. While this is cooking, beat eggs until they foam. Mix together all the ingredients and pour into pie shell. Bake at 325° for 40 minutes.

**John Barron Harris,
Texas Ranger
Association Foundation,
and wife Cheryl**

The year I was President of the Texas Pecan Growers Association we got this recipe from L.B.J.'s cook and printed it and some others to give away at the State Fair.

OPAL'S PECAN PIE

4 tablespoons butter
2 tablespoons flour
1 cup sugar
¾ cup light corn syrup
3 eggs
1 teaspoon vanilla
1 cup finely chopped pecans
1 unbaked, deep-dish pie shell

Cream the butter. Mix the flour and sugar together. Add to the butter gradually, blending thoroughly as you mix. Add the corn syrup. Beat the eggs well and stir them into the mixture. Add the vanilla. Add the pecans and stir the mixture until all the ingredients are thoroughly blended. Pour the filling into the pie shell. Bake at 200° for 1 hour or until knife inserted in the center comes out clean.

Opal Smith
Employee Texas Ranger Museum

HIGH PLAINS PECAN PIE

¾ cup sugar
2 tablespoons flour
1 teaspoon salt
½ cup maple syrup
½ cup light corn syrup
2 eggs
½ cup evaporated milk
1 teaspoon vanilla
1 cup chopped pecans
1 unbaked pie shell

In large bowl mix sugar, flour and salt. Stir in syrups. Beat in eggs. Mix in by hand the evaporated milk, vanilla and pecans. Pour into pie shell and bake at 375° about 50 minutes.

Sergeant Jim Gillespie, Company C

PECAN PIE

3 beaten eggs
1 cup sugar
1 cup light corn syrup
1 cup pecan halves
1 teaspoon vanilla
1 9-inch pie shell

Beat eggs and sugar until thick. Add corn syrup, pecans and vanilla. Pour into pie shell. Bake in oven at 300° until firm.

Sergeant Morgan L. Miller, Company D, and wife Ann

BUTTERMILK PECAN PIE

- 1½ cups sugar
- 1 tablespoon flour
- 4 tablespoons unmelted margarine
- 4 eggs
- ½ cup buttermilk
- 1 teaspoon vanilla
- 1 cup chopped pecans
- 1 9-inch unbaked pie shell

Combine sugar, flour and margarine in a bowl. Mix with electric mixer on low speed. Add eggs, 1 at a time, mixing well. Add buttermilk and vanilla. Mix well. Stir in pecans. Pour into pie shell. Bake in preheated 325° oven about 1 hour until light brown and middle is set.

**Captain Jack Dean,
Company D,
and wife Janie**

BUTTERMILK PIE

- 1¾ cups sugar
- ¼ cup flour
- ½ teaspoon salt
- 1 stick melted oleo
- ½ cup buttermilk
- 3 eggs (slightly beaten)
- 1 teaspoon vanilla

Mix flour, sugar and salt. Add melted butter and beat thoroughly. Add vanilla, buttermilk and slightly beaten eggs, mixing well. Pour into unbaked pie shell and bake at 350° for 35 minutes. Do not overbake. Remove from oven while pie is still shaky in center. This baking time is for a 9-inch pie pan.

**Sgt. Billy Peterson, Company C
and wife Barbara**

GOOD OLD "PUNKIN" PIE

- 1 cup sugar
- ½ teaspoon salt
- 1 teaspoon cinnamon
- 1 teaspoon ginger
- 1½ cups cooked pumpkin
- 2 beaten eggs
- ½ cup cream
- 1 tablespoon melted butter
- 1 unbaked pie shell

Combine dry ingredients. Add to pumpkin. Stir in eggs, then slowly add cream and butter. Pour into pie shell. Bake 10 minutes at 450°, reduce heat to 350° and bake an additional 30 to 35 minutes.

**Sergeant Jim Gillespie,
Company C**

CHEESECAKE

8 ounces cream cheese
1 can sweetened condensed milk
⅓ cup lemon juice
graham cracker crust
1 can cherry pie filling

Soften cream cheese. Mix together with sweetened condensed milk and lemon juice. Pour into crust. Top with pie filling. Quick and very good.

Sergeant Milton Wright, Company A, and wife Marian

ITALIAN CREAM CHEESE CAKE

2 cups sugar
2 sticks margarine
5 egg yolks, one at a time
1 cup buttermilk
2 cups flour
1 teaspoon soda
¼ teaspoon salt
1 teaspoon vanilla
1 cup pecans
1 cup coconut

Cream sugar, margarine and add eggs and dry ingredients. Add one cup coconut and one cup pecans. Beat egg whites and fold in. Bake in 2 cake pans and bake for 40 minutes at 350°.

Lt. Earl R. Pearson, Company F, and sister Gwenette Pearson

ITALIAN CREAM CHEESE CAKE ICING

1 box powdered sugar
1 (8 ounce) package cream cheese
1 stick margarine
1 cup pecans
1 teaspoon vanilla

Cream together and add box of powdered sugar, 1 teaspoon vanilla and 1 cup pecans. Spread on cool cake.

Lt. Earl R. Pearson, Company F, and sister Gwenette Pearson

NO BAKE CHEESECAKE

- 1 graham cracker pie crust
- 1 (8 ounce) package cream cheese, softened
- 1/3 cup sugar
- 1 cup (1/2 pint) sour cream
- 2 teaspoons vanilla
- 1 (8 ounce) carton Cool Whip, thawed

Beat cheese until smooth; gradually beat in sugar. Blend in sour cream and vanilla. Fold in whipped topping, blending well. Spoon into crust. Chill until set, at least 4 hours. Top with fresh strawberries or other fruit if desired. Preparation time: 15 minutes

Deborah Herron, Texas Ranger Association Foundation Member

BUTTERMILK COCOA CAKE

- 2 cups sugar
- 3/4 cup shortening
- 2 eggs
- 2 1/2 cups flour
- 1/2 cup cocoa
- 2 teaspoons soda
- 1 teaspoon salt
- 1 cup buttermilk
- 1 teaspoon vanilla
- 1 cup boiling water

Cream sugar and shortening. Add eggs and beat until smooth. Sift dry ingredients together and add alternately with buttermilk to creamed mixture. Add vanilla and water. Pour batter into greased and floured tube pan and bake at 350° for 1 hour or until cake springs back when touched.

Sgt. Jesse Priest, Retired

BUTTERMILK CAKE

- 2 cups flour
- 6 tablespoons cornstarch
- 1 teaspoon salt
- 6 eggs
- 3 cups sugar
- 1 cup Crisco
- 1/4 teaspoon soda
- 1 cup buttermilk
- 2 tablespoons lemon or vanilla extract

Sift flour, cornstarch and salt together and set aside. Separate eggs. Beat egg whites until stiff and set aside. Cream sugar and Crisco. Add beaten egg yolks and beat well. Add soda to buttermilk, then add alternately with flour mixture. Beat well, add flavoring. Fold in egg whites last. Pour in greased Bundt pan. Bake in preheated oven at 350° for 1 hour and 15 minutes. Do not open oven door until done.

**Edith Kidd
Texas Ranger
Association Foundation
Member**

APPLE WALNUT CAKE

1 cup butter or margarine
2 cups sugar
3 eggs
3 cups sifted, all-purpose flour
1½ teaspoons soda
½ teaspoon salt
1 teaspoon cinnamon
½ teaspoon mace
2 teaspoons vanilla
3 cups chopped apples
2 cups chopped walnuts

Cream butter and sugar until fluffy. Add eggs, one at a time, beating well after each addition. Sift together flour, soda, salt, cinnamon and mace. Add gradually to creamed mixture. Stir in vanilla, apples and walnuts. Batter will be stiff. Spoon into greased and floured 10-inch tube pan. Bake at 325° for 1½ hours. Let cool in pan 10 minutes. Remove to rack.

Captain Jack Dean,
Company D,
and wife Janie

CHOPPED APPLE CAKE

2 cups sugar
1 cup shortening
4 eggs
3 cups flour
1 teaspoon soda
½ teaspoon nutmeg
1 teaspoon cinnamon
1 teaspoon cloves
1 teaspoon salt
1 teaspoon vanilla
1 cup chopped pecans
3 cups finely chopped Winesap apples
1 cup chopped dates

Cream together sugar and shortening. Stir in eggs. Sift together dry ingredients. Add gradually to creamed mixture. Stir in vanilla. Fold in pecans and fruit. Pour into wax paper lined loaf or tube pan. Bake 3 hours at 275°.

Anonymous Texas Ranger

BANANA NUT CAKE

- 1 cup margarine
- 3 cups sugar
- 4 eggs
- 1 tablespoon vanilla
- 3 bananas
- ½ cup buttermilk
- ½ teaspoon soda
- 4 cups sifted flour
- 1 cup chopped pecans

Cream margarine and sugar. Beat in eggs separately. Add vanilla and bananas. Mix buttermilk with soda. Add alternately with flour. Stir in nuts. Line tube pan on sides and bottom with foil. Bake at 300° for 1½ hours or until done. Leave in pan 5 minutes before turning out.

Bill Nelson, Retired,
and wife Joyce

BANANA SPLIT CAKE

- 2 packages graham crackers (about 2½ cups crushed)
- ⅓ cup sugar
- 2 sticks melted margarine
- 16 ounces cream cheese
- 2 cups sugar
- 1 egg
- 1 large can drained, crushed pineapple
- 5-6 bananas
- 1 large tub frozen whipped topping
- 1 cup chopped pecans
- 1 can cherry pie filling

Crush graham crackers. Mix with ⅓ cup sugar and melted margarine. Press in 9x13x2-inch pan. Bake for 10 minutes. Beat together cream cheese, 2 cups sugar and egg. Pour over cooled crust. Spread pineapple over cream cheese mixture. Arrange sliced bananas over pineapple. Layer on topping, pecans and pie filling.

Sergeant Danny Rhea,
Company B,
and wife Sue

BROWNIE CAKE

2 cups sugar
2 cups flour
2 sticks margarine
½ cup shortening
8 tablespoons cocoa
1 cup water
¼ cup buttermilk
2 well beaten eggs
2 teaspoons vanilla
1 teaspoon soda
1 teaspoon cinnamon
6 tablespoons milk
1 box confectioner's sugar
1 cup chopped pecans

Sift sugar and flour together. Mix 1 stick margarine, shortening, 4 tablespoons cocoa and water. Bring to a boil. Pour immediately over sugar and flour mixture, stirring well. Add buttermilk, eggs, 1 teaspoon vanilla, soda and cinnamon. Mix and pour into greased 9x13-inch pan. Bake at 350° for 30 to 35 minutes. Start making icing about 5 minutes before cake is done. Melt and bring to a boil 1 stick margarine, 4 tablespoons cocoa and milk. Remove from heat and add confectioner's sugar, 1 teaspoon vanilla and pecans. Beat well and spread on cake while cake is still warm. Leave cake in pan to spread icing.

Captain Bob Mitchell, Retired,
and wife Jerry

CAKE THAT WON'T LAST

2 cups sugar
3 cups flour
1 teaspoon cinnamon
1 teaspoon salt
1 teaspoon soda
3 beaten eggs
1½ teaspoons vanilla
1½ cups oil
8 ounces crushed pineapple with juice
1 cup chopped pecans
3½ ounces coconut
8 ounces cream cheese
1 box confectioner's sugar
1 stick melted margarine
1¼ cups pecans

Combine sugar, flour, cinnamon, salt and soda in a large bowl. Add eggs, vanilla and oil. Mix well. Stir in pineapple, 1 cup pecans and coconut. Pour into pan and bake at 350° for 45 to 50 minutes. For icing mix together cream cheese and confectioner's sugar. Add margarine. Cream until smooth. Fold in 1¼ cups pecans. Add milk to make moist if necessary.

John Vickery,
Texas Ranger
Association Foundation,
and wife Patricia

CHOCOLATE CHIP CAKE

1 box yellow cake mix
1 package instant vanilla pudding
1 package instant chocolate pudding
½ cup oil
1½ cups water
4 eggs
1 cup milk chocolate chips

Mix together cake mix and pudding mixes. Add oil, water and eggs (1 at a time). Beat well. Fold in chips last. Bake in Bundt or tube pan at 350° for 50 minutes.

Captain Carl Weathers, Company C, and wife Mickey

This recipe came from Merle Moore, wife of Captain Charles Moore, of Company C.

FAVORITE CAKE

1 stick softened butter
½ cup shortening
2 cups sugar
1 teaspoon vanilla
1 teaspoon soda
5 egg yolks
1 cup buttermilk
2 cups flour
5 stiffly beaten egg whites

Cream together butter and shortening. Stir in sugar, vanilla and soda. Add egg yolks and blend well. Alternately add buttermilk and flour a little at a time. Mix well. Fold in egg whites. Bake in 3 greased and floured 9-inch pans at 350° for 20 to 25 minutes.

Captain Dan North, Retired, and wife Nancy

FAVORITE CAKE ICING

1 stick butter
1 large package cream cheese
1 teaspoon vanilla
1 box confectioner's sugar
1 can coconut
1 cup chopped pecans

Let butter and cream cheese come to room temperature. Cream together. Add vanilla, sugar, coconut and pecans. You can add a little milk if needed - just enough to help spread.

Captain Dan North, Retired, and wife Nancy

FRESH STRAWBERRY CAKE

Betty Crocker sour cream cake mix
½ cup water
½ cup oil
½ cup granulated sugar
1 package strawberry Jello
4 eggs
1 cup fresh strawberries, sliced

Mix all ingredients on medium speed until strawberries are fairly fine. Spray Bundt pan with Pam and pour in batter. Bake at 350° for 40 to 45 minutes.

Icing:
1 carton of prepared Betty Crocker Sour Cream Icing
½ to 1 cup chopped strawberries

Mix icing and strawberries. If icing is too thin, beat in powdered sugar to stiffen.

Bill Gunn, Retired, and wife Sugar

COKE CAKE

2 cups sugar
2 cups flour
2 sticks margarine
2 tablespoons cocoa
1 cup Coke
½ cup miniature marshmallows
2 eggs
½ cup buttermilk
1 teaspoon soda
1 teaspoon vanilla
1 teaspoon cinnamon
1 stick margarine
2 tablespoons cocoa
1 box confectioner's sugar
1 cup pecans

Mix sugar and flour together in large mixing bowl and set aside. Mix together and bring to a boil 2 sticks margarine, 2 tablespoons cocoa, Coke and marshmallows. Pour over sugar mixture. Add eggs, buttermilk, soda, vanilla and cinnamon. Use a spoon to mix this - not your mixer. Bake in a greased and floured tube pan at 350° until done. For frosting melt 1 stick margarine and 2 tablespoons cocoa together. Pour over confectioner's sugar. Fold in pecans. Add enough Coke to spread easily.

John Vickery, Texas Ranger Association Foundation, and wife Patricia

MEXICAN WEDDING CAKE

2 cups sugar
2 cups flour
2 teaspoons baking soda
2 beaten eggs
1 (16 ounce) can crushed pineapple (best to use pineapple in sweetened juice - makes a better cake)
1 cup shredded coconut
1 cup chopped pecans
2 teaspoons vanilla

Mix all ingredients and pour into 11x13-inch pan. Bake for 25 to 30 minutes at 350° until done. While cake is hot pour icing on cake.

Joe Davis, retired Ranger, and wife Lila

MEXICAN WEDDING CAKE ICING

1 (8 ounce) package cream cheese
1 box powdered sugar
1 stick butter
1 teaspoon vanilla

Mix until creamy and pour over hot cake.

Joe Davis, retired Ranger, and wife Lila

VANILLA WAFER CAKE

1 cup butter or margarine
2 cups sugar
6 whole eggs
1 (12 ounce) package vanilla wafers, crushed fine
½ cup milk
1 can coconut
1 can chopped pecans

Cream butter and sugar. Beat until smooth. Add eggs one at a time beating well after each addition. Add crushed vanilla wafers with milk. Add coconut and pecans. Pour into greased and floured tube pan. Bake at 270° for 1½ hours.

Edith Kidd
Texas Ranger Association Foundation Member

CINNAMON ROLL CAKE

- 1 cup sugar
- 3 tablespoons cinnamon
- 1 cup chopped pecans
- 1 package frozen parker house rolls
- 1 stick melted butter

Spray angel food cake pan with Pam. Mix sugar, cinnamon and pecans. Sprinkle 4 tablespoons of the mixture on bottom of pan. Distribute frozen rolls in pan. Sprinkle remaining sugar mixture over rolls, pour butter over top. Put in cold oven overnight. Bake in 350° oven for 45 minutes or until broom straw comes out clean.

**Bill Gunn, Retired,
and wife Sugar**

EARTHQUAKE CAKE

- 1 cup coconut
- 1 cup chopped pecans
- 1 package Swiss or German chocolate cake mix
- 8 ounces softened cream cheese
- 1 stick softened margarine
- 1 teaspoon vanilla
- 1 box confectioner's sugar

Grease a 9x13-inch cake pan. In pan bottom layer coconut and pecans. In a bowl prepare cake mix according to package directions. Pour this on top of pecans. In another bowl combine and mix well the cream cheese, margarine, vanilla and confectioner's sugar. Drop this mixture by spoonfuls into cake batter. Do not stir. Bake at 350° for 45 minutes. This is not a pretty cake (thus the name), but it is delicious.

**Sergeant Kyle Dean,
Company B**

CHOCOLATE ZUCCHINI CAKE

1 package Duncan Hines Moist Deluxe Dark Dutch cake mix
1 teaspoon ground cinnamon
3 eggs
1¼ cups water
½ cup Crisco oil
1 teaspoon vanilla
1 cup shredded zucchini

Preheat oven to 350°. Grease and flour 10-inch Bundt pan or tube pan.
Combine cake mix and cinnamon in a large bowl. Add egg, water , oil and vanilla. Beat at medium speed with electric mixer for two minutes. Stir in zucchini. Pour into pan. Bake at 350° for 50 to 60 minutes or until toothpick inserted in center comes out clean. Cool in pan 25 minutes. Invert onto serving plate. Cool completely.

Frosting:

2 (3 ounce) packages cream cheese, softened
⅓ cup butter or margarine
3½ cups confectioner's sugar
1½ teaspoons vanilla extract
1 teaspoon milk
¼ cup chopped nuts

Combine cream cheese and butter in a large bowl. Beat at medium speed with electric mixer until well blended. Add confectioner's sugar, vanilla extract and milk. Beat until smooth and creamy. Add more confectioner's sugar to thicken or milk to thin as needed. Spread on cooled cake. Sprinkle with chopped nuts. Enjoy!

Brandi Loftis, "runner"
Harris Farms

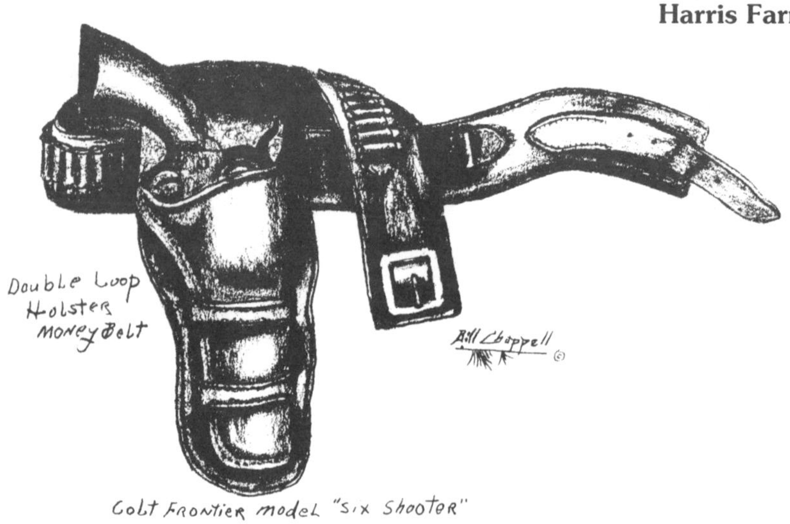

COLLECTOR'S COCOA CAKE

- ¾ cup butter
- 1¾ cups sugar
- 2 eggs
- 1 teaspoon vanilla
- 2 cups unsifted flour
- ½ cup cocoa
- 1¼ teaspoons soda
- ½ teaspoon salt
- 1½ cups water
- 1 stick margarine
- 3½ tablespoons cocoa
- ⅓ cup milk
- 1 box confectioner's sugar
- 1 cup pecans
- 1 teaspoon vanilla

Cream butter and sugar. Beat in eggs and 1 teaspoon vanilla. Combine flour, ½ cup cocoa, soda and salt. Add alternately with water to creamed mixture. Bake in floured and greased 9x13-inch pan at 350° for 35 to 40 minutes. Cool. Cake is done when it springs back when lightly touched in center. For frosting boil margarine, 3½ tablespoons cocoa and milk. After it boils remove from heat. Beat in confectioner's sugar, pecans and 1 teaspoon vanilla. Spread on cooled cake.

Sergeant Milton Wright,
Company A,
and wife Marian

CHOCOLATE SHEET CAKE

- 2 sticks margarine
- 4 tablespoons cocoa
- 1 cup Coke
- 1½ cups miniature marshmallows
- 2 cups flour
- 2 cups sugar
- ½ cup buttermilk
- 2 eggs
- 1 teaspoon soda
- 1 teaspoon vanilla
- 1 stick margarine
- 4 tablespoons cocoa
- 6 tablespoons cream
- 1 teaspoon vanilla
- 1 box confectioner's sugar

Mix together 2 sticks margarine, 4 tablespoons cocoa, Coke and marshmallows. Bring to a boil. Sift together flour and sugar. Add margarine mixture. Beat with mixer adding buttermilk, eggs, soda and vanilla. Mix well and pour in greased pan. Bake 20 minutes at 400°. For icing melt 1 stick margarine. Add 4 tablespoons cocoa and cream. Bring to a boil. Beat and add vanilla and confectioner's sugar. Pour over hot cake while still in pan.

Jim Peters, Retired,
and wife Lydia

CHOCOLATE FUDGE ICING

- 1 stick margarine
- 4 tablespoons cocoa
- 6 tablespoons milk
- 1 box confectioner's sugar
- 1 cup chopped pecans
- 1 teaspoon vanilla

Bring margarine, cocoa and milk to a boil. Take from the heat. Beat in confectioner's sugar. Add pecans and vanilla. Mix well. Frost cake while icing is still warm.

Wallace Spillar, Retired,
and wife Ann

FRUIT COCKTAIL CAKE

- 1½ cups sugar
- 2 eggs
- 2 cups flour
- 1 teaspoon salt
- 2 teaspoons soda
- 1 can fruit cocktail in juice
- ¼ cup packed brown sugar
- ½ cup chopped pecans
- 1 stick butter or margarine
- ¾ cup sugar
- ½ cup evaporated milk
- ½ cup coconut
- 1 teaspoon vanilla

Combine 1½ cups sugar, eggs, flour, salt, soda and fruit cocktail with juice. Beat well and place in greased and floured 9x13-inch pan. Sprinkle top of cake with brown sugar, then nuts. Bake in preheated oven about 30 minutes or until cake pulls away from side of pan and toothpick inserted in center comes out clean. When cake is done, combine butter, ¾ cup sugar and milk in pan on top of range. Bring to boil, stirring, then let boil for 2 minutes. Remove from heat and add coconut and vanilla. Mixture will be thin. Pour evenly over warm cake.

Sergeant W. R. "Bill" Gerth,
Company C,
and wife Dixie

ICEBOX CAKE

- **1 package Angel Food cake mix**
- **2 packages whipped topping mix**
- **1 cup sugar**
- **16 ounces softened cream cheese**

Bake cake mix according to directions. Cut cake into 4 layers. Whip whipped topping mix according to package directions. Add sugar and cream cheese. Chill. Spread between cake layers and on outside of cake. Top with topping of your choice. Keep in refrigerator.

Sergeant Danny Rhea,
Company B,
and wife Sue

Topping can be any can of pie filling. I prefer the fresh topping made of strawberry glaze and fresh berries.

MINCEMEAT CAKE

- **3/4 cup sugar**
- **1/2 cup butter**
- **1 egg**
- **1 box finely broken mincemeat**
- **1 teaspoon soda**
- **1 cup cold coffee**
- **2/3 cup molasses**
- **1 teaspoon vanilla**
- **2 cups flour**
- **1 cup pecans**

Cream sugar, butter and egg. Add mincemeat and mix well. Dissolve soda in coffee. Add coffee mixture, molasses, vanilla, flour and pecans. Bake slow at 300°.

Bill Gunn, Retired,
and wife Sugar

This recipe is one of my mother's favorites. She was the first female Deputy Sheriff of Bell County, Texas, Mrs. Ivy Mae Gunn 1905 - 1986.

JAM CAKE

1½ cups sugar
1 cup oil
1 cup jam or jelly
1 teaspoon cloves
½ teaspoon nutmeg
1 teaspoon cinnamon
3 eggs
1 cup nuts
1 teaspoon soda
½ teaspoon salt
1 teaspoon baking powder
2 cups flour
1 cup buttermilk

Mix together all ingredients. Bake at 375° for 25 to 30 minutes. Ice with confectioner's sugar icing or caramel icing.

John Barron Harris,
Texas Ranger
Association Foundation,
and wife Cheryl

This recipe belonged to my Grandmother Harris and great grandmother Sample and is over 100 years old.

BEST-EVER RUM CAKE

Take 1 to 2 quarts of rum. Before you start, sample the rum to check for quality. Good, isn't it? Now go ahead, select a large mixing bowl, measuring cup, etc. Check the rum again. It must be just right. Pour one level cup of rum into a glass and drink it as fast as you can. Repeat. With an electic mixer beat 1 cup of butter in a large fluffy bowl. Add 1 seaspoon thugar and beat again. Meanwhile, make sure that the rum is of the finest quality. Try another cup. Open second quart if necessary. Add 2 arge leggs, 2 cups fried druit and beat till high. If druit gets struck in beaters, just pry it loose with a drewscriver. Sample the rum again, checking for tonscisticity. Next sift 3 cups of pepper or salt (it really doesn't really matter which). Sample the rum again. Sift ½ pint of lemon juice. Fold in chopped butter and strained nuts. Add 1 babblespoon of brown thugar, or whatever color you can find. Wix mel. Grease oven and turn cake pan to 350 gredrees. Now pour the whole mess into the coven and ake. Check the rum again and bo to ged.

Captain Jack Dean, Company D
and Wife Janie

OATMEAL CAKE

- 1½ cups boiling water
- 1 stick margarine
- 1 cup quick oats
- 1 cup brown sugar
- 1 cup sugar
- 2 eggs
- 1⅓ cups flour
- 1 teaspoon soda
- 2 teaspoons cinnamon
- 1 stick margarine
- ¾ cup brown sugar
- ½ cup evaporated milk
- 1 cup pecans
- 1 cup coconut

Stir together water, 1 stick margarine and oats. Cover. Combine 1 cup brown sugar, sugar and eggs. Mix well. Sift together flour, soda and cinnamon. Alternate pouring oatmeal mixture and dry ingredients into sugar/egg mixture. Grease and flour a 9x13-inch pan. Bake at 350° for 30 to 35 minutes. Prepare icing while cake is baking. Heat together 1 stick margarine, ¾ cup brown sugar and milk until sugar dissolves. Add pecans and coconut. Spread on warm cake. Place under broiler and lightly brown the topping. Watch it closely, it will burn easily!

Weldon Lucas, Retired

PEANUT BUTTER CAKE

- 2 cups sifted flour
- 1⅓ cups sugar
- 2½ teaspoons baking powder
- ¾ teaspoon salt
- ½ cup softened shortening
- ⅔ cup milk
- 2 eggs
- ¼ cup milk
- 2 tablespoons peanut butter

Mix flour, sugar, baking powder and salt. Add shortening and ⅔ cup milk. Beat 2 minutes. Add eggs and ¼ cup milk. Beat 1 minute. Add peanut butter and mix well. Grease 2 8-inch layer pans. Sprinkle with flour, shaking out excess. Preheat oven to 450°. Pour batter into pans and bake. When done spread peanut butter on cake while it's hot.

Opal Smith
Employee
Texas Ranger Museum

WHACKY CAKE

- 1½ cups flour
- 1 cup sugar
- 3 tablespoons cocoa
- 1 teaspoon soda
- ½ teaspoon salt
- 1 cup cold water
- 6 tablespoons melted shortening
- 1 tablespoon vinegar
- 1 teaspoon vanilla

Sift all dry ingredients together. Add water, shortening, vinegar and vanilla. Mix well. Bake in small square pan at 350° for 20 to 25 minutes.

Buzz Dulick,
Texas Ranger
Association Foundation,
and wife Judy

For a richer cake use butter to replace shortening. For a nearly fat free cake substitute fat free mayonnaise for shortening.

POPPY SEED CAKE

- 1 package Duncan Hines butter yellow cake mix (not pudding)
- ¾ cup oil
- ½ cup sugar
- 1 teaspoon vanilla
- ¼ cup poppy seed
- 4 eggs
- 8 ounces sour cream

Combine all ingredients. Mix well. Pour into greased and floured Bundt pan. Bake 50 minutes at 350°.

Captain Bob Mitchell, Retired
and wife Jerry

DUMP CAKE

- 2 sticks butter
- 1 large can crushed pineapple
- 1 cup sugar
- 1 large can cherry pie filling
- 1 package yellow cake mix

In a 13x9-inch pan, melt 1 stick of butter. Add undrained pineapple. Sprinkle with sugar. Add cherry pie filling. Sprinkle cake mix on top. Melt second stick of butter. Drizzle on top of cake crumbs. Do not stir. Bake at 350° for 1 hour.

Sergeant Danny Rhea,
Company B,
and wife Sue

MISSISSIPPI MUD CAKE

- 4 eggs
- 2 cups sugar
- 2 sticks margarine, melted
- 1½ cups flour
- ⅓ cup cocoa
- 1 teaspoon vanilla
- 1½ cups pecans
- 1½ cups coconut
- 1 (13½ ounce) jar marshmallow creme

Beat eggs and sugar. Add margarine and mix well. Add flour and cocoa and vanilla and mix well. Stir in pecans and coconut. Bake 30 minutes (not longer) at 350°. While still hot punch holes in cake with fork. Spread marshmallow cream on top. Let cool. Frost with chocolate powdered sugar frosting.

Constance Price
Computer Expert
Harris Farms Publishing

HARRIS FARMS VANILLA ICE CREAM

- 4 eggs
- 2½ cups sugar
- 1 (14 ounce) can sweetened condensed milk
- 8 cups milk
- 1½ pints heavy whipping cream
- 2½ tablespoons vanilla
- ½ teaspoon salt

Beat eggs until light. Add sugar gradually. Beat until thick. Beat in sweetened condensed milk. Add remaining ingredients. Mix well. Freeze in gallon ice cream freezer, following manufacturer's instructions. Any chopped fruit, etc., may be added to this recipe — be creative!

John Barron Harris,
Texas Ranger
Association Foundation,
and wife Cheryl

JOHN'S BANANA ICE CREAM

- 6 over-ripe bananas
- 2 cans sweetened condensed milk
- 1 teaspoon vanilla
- 4 ripe bananas
- milk

Mix bananas, sweetened condensed milk and vanilla in blender. Pour into freezer can. Slice ripe bananas into can and fill to line with milk. Freeze according to manufacturers instructions.

John Dendy, Retired,
and wife Vineta

BANANA ICE CREAM

1¾ cups sugar
2 tablespoons flour
pinch salt
2 cups 2% milk
1 can sweetened condensed milk
4 ripe bananas
1 tablespoon vanilla
4 eggs
2% milk

In a 2-quart saucepan combine sugar, flour, and salt with 2% milk. Cook over low heat until sugar dissolves. Cool slightly. In blender, combine sweetened condensed milk, bananas and vanilla. Add to mixture in saucepan. In blender, beat eggs with a small amount of 2% milk until frothy and add to mixture. Stir well and pour into 4-quart ice cream freezer. Add 2% milk until mixture reaches the "fill line". Follow freezer instructions for making ice cream. Wrap freezer with towels and let sit for 30 to 40 minutes.

Sergeant James L. Miller,
Company F

TR'S FAMOUS ICE CREAM

3 oranges
2 lemons
1 large can apricots
1 can sweetened condensed milk
1½ cups sugar
½ pint whipping cream
1 teaspoon vanilla
milk

Squeeze juice from oranges and lemons. Blend together with apricots. Mix together sweetened condensed milk, sugar, whipping cream and vanilla. Pour into ice cream freezer. Add apricot mixture. Fill to line with milk. Freeze according to manufacturers directions.

Sergeant Tommy Ratliff,
Headquarters Company

GRAPE ICE CREAM

- 2 cans evaporated milk
- 1½ pints whipped cream
- 3 lemons
- 1 quart grape juice
- 3 cups sugar
- milk

Chill the cans of evaporated milk. Whip the evaporated milk and cream together. Squeeze the lemons. Combine the grape juice, lemon juice and sugar. Add to the whipped mixture. Pour into freezer container. Fill to line with milk and freeze according to manufacturers instructions.

Capt. Bob Prince, Retired

PECAN SANDIES

- ¾ cup shortening
- ½ cup confectioner's sugar
- 2 tablespoons water
- ½ teaspoon lemon extract
- 1½ teaspoons vanilla
- 1½ cups sifted, all-purpose flour
- chopped pecans

Cream shortening and gradually add sugar. Add water and extracts. Add flour gradually and mix well. Add pecans. Fill cookie press or roll in balls and put on ungreased cookie sheet. Press with fork. Bake at 400° for 10 to 12 minutes. Yield: 3½ dozen.

Bill Gunn, Retired,
and wife Sugar

SAND TARTS

- 1 cup softened margarine
- 3 teaspoons sugar
- 1 teaspoon vanilla
- 2¾ cups flour
- ½ cup pecans, chopped
- cherry jelly
- pecan halves

Cream together margarine, sugar and vanilla. Add flour and pecans. Form a large ball. Pinch off a small piece of dough the size of a teaspoon. Form a hole in the center and fill with a very small amount of jelly and a pecan half. Bake on ungreased cookie sheet at 350° until light brown. Let cool and roll in confectioner's sugar. Store tightly covered.

Captain W. D. Vickers,
Company A,
and wife Judy

GINGERBREAD MEN

- 2 cups molasses
- 1 tablespoon soda
- 6 cups flour
- 1 cup shortening
- 1 teaspoon ginger
- pinch of salt

Mix ingredients into a dough. Roll out on floured board, cut with cookie cutters. You may add more flour if needed. Bake at 350° for 10 to 12 minutes. (Ovens are different) Use decoration icing to decorate.

John Barron Harris, Texas Ranger Association Foundation, and wife Cheryl

This recipe belonged to my grandmother Harris and great-grandmother Sample and is over 100 years old, given to us by my Aunts Mary Frances Robert and Winnie Brown from Brazos County, Texas.

SUGAR COOKIES

- 2 beaten eggs
- ⅔ cup oil
- 2 teaspoons vanilla
- 1 teaspoon grated lemon rind
- ¾ cup sugar
- 2 cups flour
- 2 teaspoons baking powder
- ½ teaspoon salt

Combine eggs, oil, vanilla and lemon rind. Blend in sugar. Sift together flour, baking powder and salt. Stir into sugar mixture. Drop onto ungreased cookie sheet. Flatten with greased glass dipped in sugar. Bake at 400° for 8 to 10 minutes. Yield: 3 dozen.

Sergeant George L. Turner, Company F, and wife Dana

SUNFLOWER COOKIES

- 1 cup margarine
- 1 cup brown sugar
- 1 cup sugar
- 2 eggs
- 1 teaspoon vanilla
- 1½ cups flour
- ¾ teaspoon salt
- 1 teaspoon baking powder
- 3 cups regular oats
- 1 cup sunflower seed kernels

Cream margarine and sugars together. Add eggs and vanilla, beat. Add flour, salt, baking powder and oats. Blend in sunflower seed kernels. Chill dough in refrigerator for at least 15 minutes. Drop on ungreased baking sheet. Bake at 350° for 10 minutes.

Bob Connell, Retired, and wife Etta

When I shared the above cookie recipe with my mother, Lois Denson, wife of Sergeant S. H. Denson, Texas Rangers, Retired 1975, I neglected to include the word "kernels". She used whole sunflower seeds. Sarge tries very hard to eat whatever his wife cooks, but he had more than the usual difficulty with these cookies!

COWBOY COOKIES

- 2¼ cups shortening
- 2¼ cups brown sugar
- 2¼ cups sugar
- 1½ teaspoons vanilla
- 5 eggs
- 4½ cups flour
- 1⅛ teaspoons baking powder
- 2¼ teaspoons soda
- 1⅛ teaspoons salt
- 4½ cups oats
- 1 package chocolate chips
- 1 cup chopped pecans

Cream together shortening, sugars, vanilla and eggs. Sift together flour, baking powder, soda and salt. Mix together in large bowl. Add oats, chocolate chips and pecans. When well mixed, drop on greased cookie sheet with an ice cream scoop. Bake at 350° for 20 minutes or until done. Edges will be brown and center soft.

Robert C. Favor, Retired

TEXAS RANGER COOKIES

1 stick margarine
½ cup shortening
1 cup sugar
1 cup brown sugar
2 eggs
1 teaspoon vanilla
2 cups flour
1 teaspoon soda
½ teaspoon baking powder
½ teaspoon salt
2 cups quick cooking oatmeal
2 cups Rice Crispie Cereal
1 cup chopped pecans
1 cup coconut

Cream together margarine, shortening, sugar, eggs and vanilla. Sift together the flour, soda, baking powder and salt. Gradually add to the creamed mixture. Stir in the oatmeal, cereal, pecans and coconut. With a large spoon, portion out the dough. Roll into small balls and flatten on cookie sheet. Bake in a preheated 375° oven for 8 to 10 minutes.

John P. Lynch, Retired, and wife Dorothy

Sergeant Jim Gillespie, Company C

Captain Bruce M. Casteel, Headquarters Company

Sergeant John Aycock, Company F, and wife Estelle

Bill Gunn, Retired, and wife Sugar

Lucille Warren, wife of famous artist Melvin Warren

There were several Ranger Companies on special assignment on a kidnapping case. The Ranger Captain called for a conference behind an abandoned service station. One car with two Rangers in it called in saying that they were receiving fire from the kidnappers. The Captain answered and asked the Ranger if he was sure they were being fired at. The Ranger in the car came back and said, "Yes sir, but we sure would welcome a second opinion."

Bill Gunn, Retired

COWBOY RANCH COOKIES

- 1 cup shortening
- 1 cup sugar
- 1 cup brown sugar
- 2 eggs
- 2 cups flour
- 1 teaspoon soda
- ½ teaspoon baking powder
- ½ teaspoon salt
- 2 cups 3-minute oats
- 1 package chocolate chips
- 1 cup pecans
- 1 teaspoon vanilla

Cream shortening and sugars. Add eggs, beat till light and fluffy. Add dry ingredients, mix well. Add oats, chocolate chips, pecans and vanilla. Drop by teaspoon on greased cookie sheet. Bake at 350° for 13 minutes.

Sergeant Jimmy T. Hailey, Company A

CHEERY DELIGHT

- 1 can cherry pie filling
- 1 large can crushed pineapple
- 1 box white cake mix
- 1 cup melted butter or margarine
- 1 cup chopped pecans

Spray a 13x9-inch Pyrex pan with Pam. Spread pie filling in bottom of dish. Drain pineapple and spread over pie filling. Sprinkle cake mix over fruit. Drizzle melted butter over cake mix. Sprinkle top with enough pecans to cover. Bake at 350° for 1 hour or until brown.

Wilson E. Speir, and wife Ann Marie

Can add coconut and top with whipping cream or Miracle Whip when served.

BROWN SUGAR BROWNIES

- 1 pound light brown sugar
- 2 cups biscuit mix
- 4 eggs
- 1 teaspoon vanilla
- 1-2 cups chopped pecans

Combine ingredients and blend well. Pour into greased and floured 13x9-inch pan. Bake 30 to 35 minutes at 325° to 350°. Remove and cool before slicing. Dust with confectioner's sugar.

Capt. Bob Prince, Retired

CREAM CHEESE BROWNIES

- 2 packages German's Sweet chocolate
- 10 tablespoons margarine, room temperature
- 8 ounces cream cheese, room temperature
- 2 cups sugar
- 6 eggs
- 2 tablespoons flour
- 2 teaspoons vanilla
- 1 teaspoon baking powder
- ½ teaspoon salt
- 1 cup flour
- ½ teaspoon almond extract
- 1½ cups chopped nuts

Melt chocolate and 6 tablespoons butter in top of double boiler over low heat until smooth. Stir occasionally. Remove from heat; cool. In a small bowl cream remaining butter and cream cheese. Gradually add ½ cup sugar and cream until fluffy. Blend in 2 eggs, 2 tablespoons flour and 1 teaspoon vanilla. Set aside. In a large bowl, beat remaining eggs until light. Slowly add remaining sugar and beat until thick. Add baking powder, salt and 1 cup flour. Blend in chocolate mixture. Add 1 teaspoon vanilla, almond extract and 1 cup nuts. Spread ½ the chocolate mixture in a greased jelly roll pan. Top with the cream cheese mixture. Spoon on remaining chocolate. Marbelize with a knife or spoon and top with remaining nuts. Bake, being careful not to overcook. Cool completely before cutting. Use a pizza cutter to cut these in smaller squares-they're rich!

John Barron Harris,
Texas Ranger
Association Foundation,
and wife Cheryl

Be sure to read this recipe thoroughly before you attempt it. This one always gets lots of raves. Probably the best brownie recipe ever. Bon Appetit!

ONE BOWL BROWNIES

- 1 cup oil
- 6 tablespoons cocoa
- 4 eggs
- 2 cups sugar
- 2 tablespoons corn syrup
- 1 teaspoon vanilla
- 1½ cups flour
- 1 teaspoon baking powder
- 1 teaspoon salt
- 1 cup chopped pecans

Put oil in a bowl. Stir in cocoa, eggs, sugar, syrup and vanilla. Mix flour, baking powder and salt together. Add to cocoa mixture. Stir in pecans. Pour into greased 8x12-inch pan and bake at 350° for 30 minutes. If a glass pan is used, bake at 325°. They are chewier if not overbeaten or overbaked.

Billy Crawford,
Director Texas Ranger
Association Foundation
and wife

These brownies have been the primary dessert addition to "cowboy" lunch boxes on the McBride ranch in Llano for some 30 years.

ENGLISH TRIFLE

- 1 box nut bread mix
- ¼ cup orange juice
- 1 large box instant vanilla pudding
- 1 large tub frozen whipped topping
- 1 jar preserves
- ½ cup chopped pecans

Prepare nut bread according to package directions. Crumble bread in bowl and pour orange juice over it. Refrigerate for 2 hours. Prepare pudding according to package directions. Mix with whipped topping. Layer bread in a large bowl with preserves (I prefer apricot), then the whipped topping mixture. Continue layering until bowl is full. Put remaining whipped topping on top and sprinkle with nuts. Place in refrigerator overnight or for several hours before serving.

Sergeant Donald R. Morris,
Company A,
and wife Phyllis

CHOCOLATE TRIFLE

1 large angel food cake
2 large boxes instant chocolate pudding
2 cans cherry pie filling pecans
½ pint whipping cream

Cut ½ of angel food cake into small pieces. Mix 1 package of instant pudding according to directions. Pour immediately over cake while pudding is thin. After pudding firms, add 1 can cherry pie filling, sprinkle with nuts. Add thin layer of whipped cream. Repeat layers to fill bowl. Top with whipped cream.

Captain Jack Dean,
Company D,
and wife Janie

Use a trifle bowl or another clear glass bowl to show layers.

BRAZOSBERRY COBBLER

4 cups Brazosberries
2½ cups water
4 teaspoons tapioca
2 cups sugar
½ teaspoon almond extract
3 drops red food coloring

Mix all ingredients in a very large Corningware baking dish. Prepare a double batch of pastry. Roll out half the pastry, cutting it into about 1-inch squares. Stir the squares into the cobbler mix. Roll out the rest of the pastry and cut into ½-inch strips. Form these into a lattice top for the cobbler. Sprinkle a little sugar and nutmeg on top. Bake at 325° for 45 minutes or until the top crust is a light brown. Serve hot. Great with whipped cream, Blue Bell Homemade Vanilla ice cream or evaporated milk, which is an old Connell custom.

Bob Connell, Retired,
and wife Etta

In an emergency dewberries may be substituted for Brazosberries. Brazosberries may be obtained from Bob's garden.

HILL COUNTRY COBBLER

- **8 cups peeled and sliced fresh peaches**
- **2 cups sugar**
- **2-4 tablespoons flour**
- **½ teaspoon ground nutmeg**
- **⅓ cup melted butter or margarine**
- **2 9-inch unbaked pie shells**

Preheat oven to 475°. In large pan, combine peaches, sugar, flour and nutmeg. Bring to a boil and cook over low heat 10 minutes or until tender. Remove from the heat and add butter. Spoon half of the peaches into a 9x13-inch buttered baking dish and top with pie shell. Bake for 12 minutes or until golden brown. Remove from oven and spoon remaining peaches over baked pastry. Cut remaining pastry into ½-inch strips. Arrange in lattice design over peaches. Brush strips with melted butter and sprinkle with sugar. Return to oven for 10 to 15 minutes. Serves 8.

Captain Jack Dean, Company D, and wife Janie

PEACH COBBLER

- **1½ cups sugar**
- **2 cups peaches**
- **¾ cup flour**
- **2 teaspoons baking powder**
- **¾ cup milk**
- **1 stick butter**

Sprinkle ¾ cup sugar over fruit. Let stand. Make batter of flour, ¾ cup sugar, baking powder and milk. Melt 1 stick butter in baking dish. Pour in batter, then peaches, mix well. Bake at 350° for 1 hour.

Wallace Spillar, Retired, and wife Ann

WASHDAY COBBLER

- 1 stick butter or margarine
- 2 cups sugar
- ¾ cup milk
- 1 cup flour
- 2 teaspoons baking powder
- ⅛ teaspoon salt
- 2-4 cups fruit or berries

Heat oven to 350°. Melt margarine in 9x13-inch dish. In separate bowl mix 1 cup sugar, milk, flour, baking powder and salt. Pour over melted margarine. If using canned fruit, drain. Top flour mixture with fruit and sprinkle with remaining cup of sugar. Bake for 30 to 45 minutes until crust is golden.

Glenn Krueger, and wife Jackie

This recipe belongs to my son in Del Rio, Texas, Richard A. Krueger. We made this with fresh peaches from his trees and it is delicious.

THE OLD PANTRY

It stood next to the kitchen,
Only a door between;
It held the many goodies
About which children dream;

Sweet jellies, red and purple,
(Wild strawberry and grape);
Fresh pies and homemade cookies
And tasty chocolate cake.

It stood next to the kitchen,
With just a door between...
The old pantry at Grandma's
Where goodies reigned supreme.

Glenn Krueger and Wife Jackie

QUICK PEACH COBBLER

- 1 large can peach halves
- allspice
- cinnamon
- 1 cup flour
- 1 cup sugar
- ½ stick margarine

Spray 9x9x3-inch baking dish with Pam. Drain peaches, reserving juice. Place peaches in bottom of dish with pit side up. Cover the bottom of the pan. Sprinkle peaches with allspice and cinnamon to taste. Mix flour and sugar. Pour over peaches. Pour juice gently over the entire mixture. Cut margarine in pieces and place evenly over entire dish. Place in preheated 350° oven and cook till brown on top.

John Dendy, Retired, and wife Vineta

VINEGAR COBBLER

- 1½ tablespoons flour
- 2 cups sugar
- 1 teaspoon cinnamon
- 2 cups water
- ½ cup white vinegar

Mix dry ingredients in a glass casserole bowl. Add water and vinegar. Make short biscuit dough or use biscuit mix with ¾ cup sugar mixed in. Roll out like a cinnamon roll; brush with melted butter, sugar and cinnamon. Slice ½-inch thick slices; arrange on top of vinegar mixture. Bake at 350° to 375° till dough is done and juice is thickened. Take the first bite, and if it makes you want to blow through your nose like a horse, you went a little heavy on the vinegar!

Clayton Mckinney, Retired

EASY COBBLER

- ½ cup butter or margarine
- 1 cup sugar
- 1 cup flour
- 3 teaspoons baking powder
- ½ teaspoon salt
- 1 cup milk
- 1 quart fruit

Melt butter in bottom of oblong pan. Mix together sugar, flour, baking powder, salt and milk. Pour batter over margarine. Pour fruit on top of batter. Bake at 325° until crust rises and browns. This cobbler is good with blackberries.

Sergeant Donald R. Morris,
Company A,
and wife Phyllis

BANANA PUDDING

- 1½ cups sugar
- ½ teaspoon salt
- 5 tablespoons flour
- 4 cups milk
- 2 tablespoons vanilla
- 6 well beaten eggs
- 4 bananas
- vanilla wafers

Put all dry ingredients in large pan. Add milk, vanilla and eggs. Cook on medium heat. Stir the whole time you are cooking (approximately 14 minutes) until right thickness. Add bananas and put in bowl lined with vanilla wafers.

Captain Carl Weathers,
Company C,
and wife Mickey

This is one of our favorite breakfasts for when we have company. It has eggs, milk, fruit and "cereal" - a complete meal. We always eat this pudding while still warm, but it is also good cold if there is anything left over.

BREAD PUDDING

- 2 cups milk
- ½ stick margarine
- 5 slices bread, crumbled
- 1 cup sugar
- 1 teaspoon vanilla
- 1 teaspoon cinnamon
- 1 teaspoon nutmeg
- 1 cup raisins

Warm milk and margarine together. Mix all ingredients and bake at 425° for 25 minutes.

Toliver H. Dawson, Retired

CHEF LEE'S BREAD PUDDING

- 3 beaten eggs
- 1½ cups sugar
- 2 tablespoons brown sugar
- 1 tablespoon vanilla
- ½ teaspoon nutmeg
- ½ stick melted margarine
- 3 cups heavy cream
- dash yellow food coloring
- 4 cups cubed day-old white bread
- ¾ cup raisins

Combine eggs, sugars, vanilla and nutmeg. Add melted margarine, then cream, then coloring and mix well. Stir in cubed bread and raisins and let stand 10 to 15 minutes. Pour into well greased deep pan or casserole. Bake at 375° for 45 to 60 minutes, until golden brown. Serve warm, topped with Butter Vanilla Sauce.

Captain Jack Dean,
Company D,
and wife Janie

BUTTER VANILLA SAUCE

- 1 beaten egg
- 3 tablespoons brown sugar
- ½ cup sugar
- 2 tablespoons melted butter
- 1 tablespoon flour
- 1 teaspoon vanilla
- dash nutmeg
- 1¼ cups heavy cream

Combine all ingredients in the top of a double boiler. Cook, stirring until thickened. Serve over Chef Lee's Bread Pudding.

Captain Jack Dean,
Company D,
and wife Janie

ICE BOX BANANA PUDDING

- 2 small boxes instant vanilla pudding
- 3 cups milk
- 1 can sweetened condensed milk
- 1 small carton frozen whipped topping
- vanilla wafers
- 6 bananas

Beat pudding and milk together for 2 minutes. Add sweetened condensed milk, mix well. Fold in whipped topping. Layer wafers, bananas and pudding in a 13x9-inch Pyrex pan. Top with crumbled wafers. Refrigerate.

Phil Ryan, Retired

VIRGINIA STRAWBERRY MOLD

- 1 pound butter or oleo
- 2 cups sugar
- 3 egg whites
- ½ cup sugar
- 1 quart strawberries, cut in fourths
- 1 cup nuts
- 2 cups vanilla wafer crumbs

Cream butter or oleo with sugar. Cream well. Beat eggs whites stiff and add sugar. Fold egg whites into butter mixture and add strawberries. Add nuts. Put a layer of vanilla wafer crumbs, then a layer of butter mixture. Make three layers of each. This is delicious.

**John Barron Harris,
Texas Ranger
Association Foundation,
and wife Cheryl**

The recipe came originally from my cousin - Artie Frances Bullock White. This is one of the best desserts I have ever tasted. J.H.

PINEAPPLE ICE BOX LOAF

- ½ cup butter
- 1½ cups sugar
- 4 egg yolks
- 1 large can crushed pineapple
- vanilla wafers

Cream butter well, add sugar gradually, add egg yolks one at a time and beat well after each one. Add pineapple, then fold in egg whites, which have been beaten stiff. Put layer of vanilla wafers, then cover with above mixture, another layer of vanilla wafers and continue until all of above mixture has been used. Let set in ice box, at least over night. Cover with foil. Very good and easy. One of my favorites when I was growing up.

**John Barron Harris,
Texas Ranger
Association Foundation,
and wife Cheryl**

One of my favorites when I was growing up. This one is from my 92 year old mother, Artie Harris who is a wonderful cook!

HONEY BEE BARS

1 cup sugar
2 cups flour
1 teaspoon soda
1 teaspoon cinnamon
1 beaten egg
1½ cups finely chopped pecans
¼ cup honey
¾ cup oil
1 cup sifted confectioner's sugar
½ teaspoon vanilla
1 tablespoon mayonnaise
1½ tablespoons water

Mix together sugar, flour, soda, cinnamon, egg and pecans. Add honey and oil. Mix only until ingredients are blended. Spread on cookie sheet and bake at 350° for 12 minutes. For glaze mix together confectioner's sugar, vanilla, mayonnaise and water. Beat until blended. Spread on hot bars. Yield: 24 - 2½-inch squares.

Jack Van Cleve, Retired, and wife La Vane

CHEESE CRUNCHIES

12 ounces butterscotch morsels
6 tablespoons butter
2 cups graham cracker crumbs
2 cups chopped pecans
16 ounces softened cream cheese
½ cup sugar
4 eggs
¼ cup flour
2 tablespoons lemon juice

Mix butterscotch morsels and butter in large bowl over hot water until melted and smooth. Add crumbs and pecans to mixture with a fork until it resembles pie dough. Save 2 cups of mixture for the top. Press the rest into a greased 15x10x1-inch pan and bake at 350° for 12 minutes. Combine cream cheese and sugar, beat until creamy. Add eggs one at a time. Blend in flour and lemon juice. Pour over crust, sprinkle with the 2 cups of crumb mixture. Bake at 350° for 25 minutes. Cool and chill before serving. Cut into 1-inch squares.

Captain Carl Weathers, Company C, and wife Mickey

This recipe came from Nancy North, wife of Captain Dan North, Retired of Company A.

PEANUT BUTTER FUDGE

- 2 sticks margarine
- ½ cup milk
- 5-6 tablespoons cocoa
- 2 teaspoons vanilla
- dash salt
- 2 pounds confectioner's sugar
- 1½ cups peanut butter

Microwave margarine for 2 minutes in a medium size bowl. Add milk, cocoa, vanilla, salt and confectioner's sugar. Stir well. Microwave mixture for 2 more minute. Add peanut butter, stir well. Pour into oblong cake pan and eat now or cool and eat later.

**Captain Carl Weathers,
Company C,
and wife Mickey**

When my family asks me if I have 4 minutes, I know what they want me to make.

MILLIONAIRE FUDGE

- 4½ cups sugar
- 1 large can evaporated milk
- ¾ stick butter
- 3 packages chocolate chips
- 1 jar marshmallow creme
- 2 cups pecans
- 2 teaspoons vanilla
- pinch salt

In large saucepan combine sugar, milk and butter. Cook 6 minutes after it starts to boil. Add chocolate chips, marshmallow creme, pecans, vanilla and salt. Pour into buttered 9x13-inch pan. Let cool.

**Sergeant Milton Wright,
Company A,
and wife Marian**

PRALINES

- ½ pint whipping cream (not whipped)
- 1 box brown sugar
- 3 cups pecans (halves or pieces)

Mix whipping cream and brown sugar and cook over medium heat to soft ball stage. Remove from heat, stir in pecans and heat a few minutes. Drop by teaspoon onto waxed paper. Let cool.

**Ranger L. T. Carpenter, retired,
and wife Jean**

ORIGINAL MEXICAN PRALINES

Put 3 cups of whole halves of shelled pecans, 3 cups of sugar and about ¾ to 1 cup of water (sprinkle a few grains of salt if you desire) in large saucepan. Bring to a boil, boil to thread stage. Pour in about ¼ cup of water (no more...the water you add is just enough to stop the boiling). Bring mixture to thread stage again. Pour in about ¼ cup of water (no more) and bring it to thread again. Now, once more, add a little of the water (no more) and let come to thread again. If you want sugary or grainy pralines, stir often...for creamy pralines, don't stir so much. Remove from heat and stir a few minutes; do not over beat. While still hot and syrupy, pour out the pralines by tablespoonfuls (4 to 6 pecan halves) with a little of the sugary syrup over them.

Rhoda Willeford

Practice makes perfect!

PEANUT BRITTLE

1 cup peanuts
1 cup sugar
½ cup white corn syrup
⅛ teaspoon salt
1 teaspoon butter or margarine
1 teaspoon vanilla
1 teaspoon soda

Stir together peanuts, sugar, syrup and salt in a 1½-quart casserole. Place in microwave and cook 7 to 8 minutes, stirring well. After 4 minutes, add butter and vanilla and stir well. Return to microwave and cook for an additional 1 to 2 minutes. Peanuts will be lightly browned and syrup very hot. Add soda and gently stir until light and foamy. Pour mixture onto lightly greased baking sheet. Allow to cool for ½ to 1 hour.

Captain Bob Mitchell, Retired, and wife Jerry

BUTTER CREAM MINTS

- **8 ounces softened cream cheese**
- **¼ teaspoon oil of peppermint**
- **½ teaspoon butter extract cake coloring**
- **2 pounds confectioner's sugar**

Cream cheese with oil of peppermint and butter extract. Do not use peppermint extract! Let rest in bowl covered with a plate. Remove a small amount and add desired color. Slowly add confectioner's sugar. Knead until it is "just right". It must not be on the sticky side, if so, add more sugar. Pinch off marble-sized dabs and roll. Push into decorative molds. You may need to dip them into sifted confectioner's sugar and dust them off before mashing them into molds. When finished, flip them out on waxed paper and let dry 3 or 4 hours (or longer depending on firmness). Turn over and let other side dry for another 3 to 4 hours. These may be made into round coin sized mints without using the molds. These keep excellently and freeze nicely. Store in an air-tight Tupperware or similar container. Yield: 150 to 175 "rose" mints.

Rhoda Willeford

BOURBON BALLS

- **1 package finely crushed vanilla wafers**
- **1 cup confectioner's sugar**
- **1 cup finely chopped pecans**
- **¼ cup light corn syrup**
- **2 tablespoons cocoa**
- **½ cup bourbon**
- **½ cup sugar**

In large bowl thoroughly mix all ingredients except sugar. Shape into 1-inch balls. Roll in sugar. Store in tightly covered container for at least 3 days before serving to allow flavors to mellow. Keeps up to 2 weeks. Do not freeze. Yield: 3½ dozen balls. 85 calories each.

Anonymous, Texas Ranger

BANANA SPLIT DESSERT

- 2 cups graham cracker crumbs
- 1 stick melted margarine
- 2 eggs
- 8 ounces cream cheese
- 2 cups confectioner's sugar
- 4-6 sliced bananas
- 1 large can crushed pineapple
- 1 large tub frozen whipped topping
- 1 cup chopped pecans

Mix graham cracker crumbs and margarine. Pat down in 9x13-inch pan. Beat together eggs, cream cheese and confectioner's sugar. Spread over crust. Layer on bananas, pineapple, whipped topping and pecans. Refrigerate overnight. Serves 8.

Anonymous, Texas Ranger

COCONUT CRESCENTS

- ½ cup milk
- ½ cup water
- 4½ cups flour
- 1 teaspoon salt
- ½ cup sugar
- 2 packages yeast
- 6 tablespoons butter
- 2 beaten eggs
- 1 cup coconut
- 1 cup brown sugar
- ½ cup softened butter
- 4 tablespoons flour
- ⅔ cup chopped pecans

Heat milk and water in saucepan. Combine 1 cup flour, salt, sugar and yeast. Add milk and water mixture. Beat until smooth. Add remaining flour, 6 tablespoons butter and eggs. Knead until smooth. Let rise to double in bulk. Roll into circles and cut in pie-shaped wedges. In small bowl combine coconut, brown sugar, ½ cup butter, 4 tablespoons flour and pecans. Mix well. Add filling to crust. Roll to make crescents starting with wide side. Let rise again until double in bulk. Bake at 375° for 12 to 15 minutes.

**Sergeant Milton Wright,
Company A,
and wife Marian**

Little smokies may be substituted for the coconut filling to make sausage roll-ups.

CHOCOLATE DELIGHT

1 cup flour
1 stick melted butter
1 cup chopped pecans
1½ cups sugar
2½ tablespoons flour
2 tablespoons cocoa
2 egg yolks
1½ cups milk
1 teaspoon vanilla
1 tablespoon butter
8 ounces cream cheese
1 cup confectioner's sugar
1 cup frozen whipped topping

Mix 1 cup flour, 1 stick butter and pecans in 13x9-inch oblong pan. Press down on bottom and slightly on sides. Bake at 325° until golden brown. Do not overbake. Cool completely. Mix sugar, 2½ tablespoons flour and cocoa. Add egg yolks and milk. Mix and cook on medium heat until thick, stirring constantly. After cooked, add vanilla and 1 tablespoon butter. Mix together and set aside. Allow to cool completely. In a large mixing bowl add cream cheese. Use electric mixer and gradually add the confectioner's sugar until well blended. Add whipped topping and blend. After crust is completely cooled add the cream cheese layer on top of crust and spread evenly. Next, add the chocolate filling on top of cream cheese, spreading evenly. Refrigerate for at least 2 hours. Before serving top with additional whipped topping.

Sergeant Barry K. Caver, Company A

Circa 1864-1870
Note fronts were made in one piece.

PINK STUFF

- 1 can cherry pie filling
- 5 ounces crushed pineapple
- 1 can sweetened condensed milk
- ¼ cup lemon juice
- 1 large carton frozen whipped topping

Mix all ingredients together in a bowl. Serve.

**Sergeant Milton Wright,
Company A,
and wife Marian**

Some of my family likes this as a dessert and others as a salad.

Rangers going on a Scout, 1880's or 1890's.

A RANGER'S STORY

There were several Ranger companies on special assignment on a kidnapping case. Captain Bob Mitchell called for a conference behind an abandoned service station. Ranger Joe Wilie (now a captain), called in saying that they were receiving fire from kidnappers. Captain Mitchell answered and asked if he was sure they were being fired on. Joe's reply was, "Yes sir, but we sure would welcome a second opinion!"

Captain Bob Mitchell
Co. F, retired

Rangers on back row with captured prisoners on front.
Captain Bill McDonald on far right of back row.

★ ★ ★ ★

Fireside Fixin's

Photograph courtesy of Archives Division - Texas State Library

Old time Ranger cooking ribs.

GOVERNOR JAMES V. ALRED

In the early 1900's, the Ranger service fell on hard times due to political corruption in the Governor's office. Adjutant General Sterling quit and 40 Rangers went with him. Governor Maw Ferguson cut the pay and expense money so badly that the service fell to 32 people. The next day after her pay cut she fired everyone who had not quit the day before. She then appointed her own people, which included a lot of questionable characters. She made over 2000 special appointments including some to ex-convicts and known criminals.

In 1935 Governor James V. Alred took office. One of his first acts was to cancel all special Ranger commissions. The Rangers were then put in a new department called the Department of Public Safety. At this time the Rangers were divided into five districts. The Governor could no longer make appointments and Rangers were selected by the Director of the DPS and a three member Public Safety Commission.

Governor Alred was a fine looking young man and pledged to reform. He campaigned extensively all over Texas and was a great orator. I was a very young boy and not old enough to vote, but I encouraged all my family to vote for Jimmy Alred. He made a speech one night at Kurten, Texas in Brazos County while he was standing on the back of a wagon. I was so small I had to get all the way to the front in order to see or hear him. I was convinced if he was elected Governor, Texas would never see another 'bad off' day. He quoted the poem 'Cattle' with such force that I could almost hear the lowing herds. I went home and learned the poem and am including it here for you to read.

Gov. James V. Alred with a group of Texas Rangers in 1936.

CATTLE

Other states were carved or born,
Texas grew from hide and horn,

Other states are long or wide,
Texas is a shaggy hide,

Dripping blood and crumpled hair;
Some fat giant flung it there,

Laid the head where valleys drain,
Stretched its rump along the plain.

Other soil is full of stones,
Texans plow up cattle-bones.

Herds are buried on the trail,
Underneath the powdered shale;

Herds that stiffened like the snow,
where the icy northers go.

Other states have built their halls,
Humming tunes along the walls.

Texans watched the mortar stirred,
While they kept the lowing herd.

Stamped on Texas wall and roof
Gleams the sharp and crescent hoof.

High above the hum and stir
Jingle bridle-rein and spur.

Other states were made or born,
Texas grew from hide and horn.

Bertha Hart Nance

CAPTAIN JOHN HUGHES

Captain John Hughes is generally accepted as being the model for the original fictional Lone Ranger. George W. Trendle created the character in 1932 and he was very popular on radio, in the movies and in comic books. To some extent he is still popular today because of (television) reruns. Zane Grey also used Hughes as the model for his character in his book, "The Lone Ranger".

John R. Hughes was born February 11, 1855 in Henry Country, Illinois. At the age of 14 he left home to work on a ranch, but soon left for the Indian Territory. He lived with the Choctaw and Osage for four years before moving to the Comanche nation. He was a trader around Fort Sill and was a friend of Quanah Parker, the last great Comanche Chief. After six years, Hughes bought a farm near Liberty Hill in Travis County, Texas.

In 1886 Hughes set out to find horse thieves that had stolen horses from him and his neighbors and finally tracked them to New Mexico. He killed or captured them, bringing the horses back to Texas. This caught the attention of the Texas Rangers as well as an outlaw gang called "The Wild Bunch" led by Butch Cassidy. Hughes was persuaded to join the Rangers and was sworn in on August 10, 1887. He was stationed at Camp Wood, Texas, with Company D which was a frontier battalion. He served mainly along the border of Texas and Mexico. He became known as the "Border Boss".

When the old Company D border battalion was abolished in 1900 he was made Captain of the new Company D and was later appointed Senior Captain stationed at Austin, Texas. In 1915, having served as a Captain in the Rangers longer than any other man at that time, he retired.

He was the Chairman of the Board of the Citizens Industrial Bank of Austin and the largest single stockholder, but kept his residence in El Paso, Texas. He was the first recipient of the Certificate of Valor in 1940. This is a peace officer award set up to call attention to the bravery of peace officers throughout the nation. Hughes never married, but always liked female companionship. He spent his later years traveling around the country. He once said if he ever got to the point where he didn't want female companionship he would do himself in. He died of a gunshot wound in Austin, Texas on June 3, 1947.

*Poem written by Captain Hughes in 1927

When my old soul hunts range and rest
Beyond the last divide,
Just plant me in some strip of west,
That's sunny, lone and wide.

Let cattle rub my headstone round,
And coyotes wail their kin,
Let horses come and paw the mound,
But don't you fence it in.

MEXICAN CHICKEN

- 1 chicken
- 1 chopped onion
- ½ pound pasteurized process cheese spread
- 1 teaspoon garlic salt
- 1 teaspoon chili powder
- ½ can diced tomatoes and green chilies
- 1 package tortillas
- 2 cans cream of chicken soup

Boil chicken, cut in bite size pieces. Reserve stock. Mix chicken, onion, cheese, garlic salt, chili powder and tomatoes and green chilies. Soften tortillas in boiling stock. Line in 9x13-inch baking dish. Add chicken mixture. Pour soup over mixture and bake at 350° for 35 minutes or until bubbly and hot.

Sergeant Milton Wright,
Company A,
and wife Marian

To make it hot, use the full can of tomatoes and green chilies. If more liquid is needed, add ½ cup stock.

BEER-IN-THE-REAR-CHICKEN

Buy a whole frying-size chicken. This will work equally well on the BBQ pit or in the kitchen oven. You can prepare the chicken to suit individual tastes. You are limited only by your imaginations. Some suggestions are to rub the chicken with olive oil and sprinkle with rosemary and thyme, or sprinkle with onion flakes and garlic flakes (inside and out). Place slice of onion, apple or celery in cavity of the chicken. After preparing chicken open a can of light beer (removing tab and opening one or two additional holes) and insert can of beer upright into cavity of the chicken and place upright in shallow pan in oven at 325° 2 hours or until done. If BBQing place chicken upright on grill (after placing beer can in cavity). Baste with sauce about 30 minutes before done.

Bill Gunn, Retired,
and wife Sugar

Don't cook just one - there won't be enough to go around!
When Bill Gunn first introduced us to this recipe, we had our doubts. We could not imagine it was so easy and sooo good. Before we had a chance to try it out, a friend, Bob Weber, asked us over to eat one night. On the pit along with the beef he was cooking were whole chickens which were standing upright on beer cans. They were ready to come off the grill before the beef. He had slit the skins and put seeded quarters of jalapeños between the skin and meat. Then he had rubbed dry Hidden Valley dressing mix all over the chicken for seasoning and set each chicken on a can of beer on the pit. It was some of the best chicken we have ever eaten.

The Rangers have a long history of campouts and cooking their own meals. As in any organization if one person excels as a cook then he is usually given the job. Company F of Waco, Texas was no different. The Ranger who was Company F's cook was none other than George Roach, a large man with a huge appetite.

In 1961 I was still considered a "rookie Ranger", even though I had in four years. It was this year when I learned to appreciate George's knowledge of preparing a hot meal. In September, 1961, hurricane "Carla" blew into Texas' Galveston coast with a vengeance.

Captain Clint Peoples assigned George and me to Company A in Houston to work this area - protecting life and property. So as we left Waco George advised me we needed supplies. Pooling our money George purchased the supplies and I was amazed at some of the things he bought. Being a rookie I kept quiet for George was an old timer and I respected his judgment.

We arrived in Houston and "Carla" blew through. Captain Khevenhagen assigned George and me to Palacios, Texas. The first day out we were crossing the area and I was wondering about supper. About 2:00 PM, we pulled off the road. George got out, opened the trunk and took out a nice piece of beef from the supply box. He placed it in a piece of foil and basted it with his special seasoning he had brought from Stephenville. He added some cut up onions and potatoes and then rolled the makings up.

I stood watching in amazement and trying to figure out how George was going to cook this roast. He said, "Johnny, open the hood of this car." He placed the roast on the engine, closed the hood and stated "Let's go. We'll have supper at 7:00 PM." About 6:30 PM we stopped the car. George retrieved the roast opening the foil, and we had one of the best meals I had for many moons. I believe George's seasoning made the difference. That's another story.

Sergeant Johnny Krumnow, Retired

FRIED CHICKEN

Heat oven to 425° to 450°. Cut up and skin chicken. Put flour, salt, pepper and onion powder in plastic bag. Melt 1 stick of margarine or butter in cake pan. Wash chicken and put wet chicken in bag of flour. Close bag and shake well. Roll chicken in melted margarine. Place in oblong cake pan. Put in oven and bake 45 minutes to 1 hour. You can just forget chicken or you can turn it about half way through cooking time. Do not cover chicken. I also put on a pan of potatoes to mash and open a can of green beans to warm slowly while chicken is cooking. When chicken is done you use leftover flour to make gravy in same pan you cooked chicken in. I do this on stove burner.

Captain Carl Weathers,
Company C,
and wife Mickey

My mother-in-law gave me this one and it is the easiest way to fry chicken. No mess either. For a working woman it is nice to get started and go rest for a while. I also cook steaks, pork chops and deer steaks this way, just not as long.

OVEN-FRIED CHICKEN

1 chicken
½ cup sour cream
1 tablespoon lemon juice
1 teaspoon Worcestershire sauce
1 teaspoon salt
dash black pepper
½ teaspoon paprika
2 cloves minced garlic
1 teaspoon celery salt
1 cup dry breadcrumbs or cracker crumbs
2 tablespoons margarine

Heat oven to 350°. Cut chicken into serving pieces. Combine all ingredients except breadcrumbs and margarine. Dip chicken in mixture and then into breadcrumbs. Melt margarine in large foil-lined pan. Arrange chicken (skin side down) in pan. Bake for 45 to 60 minutes or until tender and crusty brown. Do not turn chicken.

Sergeant Gary Henderson,
Company F,
and wife Sally

CHICKEN DELICIOUS

8 chicken breasts, skinned and boned
8 slices Swiss cheese
1 can cream of chicken soup
¾ cup dry white wine
1 cup herb-flavor croutons
¼ cup melted margarine

Lay chicken breasts in oblong pan. Lay 1 slice of cheese on each breast. Mix soup and wine together and spoon on top of each breast. Crush croutons and sprinkle over top. Pour melted margarine over mixture and bake at 350° for 55 to 60 minutes.

Lloyd Johnson, Retired

CHICKEN RICE CASSEROLE

1½ cups uncooked rice
1 package onion soup mix
4 cans water
1 can cream of mushroom soup
salt and pepper
1 skinned, cut-up chicken
½ stick margarine

In 9x11-inch pan, mix uncooked rice with onion soup. In bowl, mix four cans water with mushroom soup and pour over rice and onion soup mixture. Salt and pepper chicken pieces and place in pan. Top with margarine. Cover with foil and cook for approximately 1 hour at 350°.

Jim Peters, Retired,
and wife Lydia

This is also very good fixed with pork chops instead of chicken. Adding a can of mushroom pieces adds a little "extra".

CHICKEN TORTILLA CASSEROLE

5 whole chicken breasts
1 can cream of chicken soup
1 can cream of mushroom soup
1 cup sour cream
1 (6 ounce) can pitted ripe olives, drained
1 (4 ounce) can whole green chilies, seeded and chopped
1 chopped onion
6 corn tortillas, cut into ½-inch strips
10 ounces sharp Cheddar cheese, shredded

Poach chicken until tender. Cool, then bone and cut into bite size pieces. Blend soups and cream. Mix with olives, chiles and onion. Spread a small amount of sauce on bottom of 2½-quart casserole. Arrange a layer of tortilla strips, followed by layers of chicken, sauce and cheese. Repeat as necessary. Top with cheese. Cover with foil and bake in a preheated oven at 350° for 45 minutes, or until bubbly.

Alva Stem, Retired Director of Parks and Recreation Department City of Waco, and wife Helen, Foundation Members

CHICKEN LOAF

4 tablespoons melted margarine
4 tablespoons flour
2 cups milk
3 cubes chicken bouillon
2 eggs
1 cup mayonnaise
2 cups cooked, cubed chicken
1 can Chinese noodles
½ cup almonds
3 tablespoons margarine
1 can drained mushrooms
1 can cream of celery soup

Mix together 4 tablespoons margarine, flour, milk and bouillon cubes. Cook until thick. Add gradually to eggs. Mix with mayonnaise, chicken, noodles and almonds. Pour into greased baking dish and cook 50 to 60 minutes at 350°. Combine 3 tablespoons margarine, mushrooms and soup for sauce.

Capt. Bob Prince, Retired

COUNTRY CHICKEN DELITE

- 2 packages broccoli spears
- 1½ cups chicken broth
- 1 can cream of mushroom soup
- ¼ cup melted margarine
- 1½ cups breadcrumbs
- 1½ cups grated Cheddar cheese
- 1 chicken, cooked and boned

Cook broccoli according to package directions. Mix broth and soup together. Pour margarine over breadcrumbs. Lay broccoli spears on bottom of greased 9x13-inch casserole dish. Spread cheese over broccoli. Layer on the chicken in large chunks. Pour on the soup mixture. Sprinkle breadcrumb mixture on top. Bake at 350° for 30 minutes or until breadcrumbs are brown. May be prepared in advance and frozen. Serves 4 to 6.

H. R. "Lefty" Block, Retired, and wife

CHICKEN & BROCCOLI

- 2 packages frozen broccoli
- 2 cups cooked chicken
- 2 cans cream of chicken soup
- 1 cup mayonnaise
- 1 tablespoon lemon juice
- ½ cup grated longhorn cheese

Cook broccoli until tender. Arrange in bottom of casserole dish. Cut chicken into bite size pieces. Place on top of broccoli. Combine soup, mayonnaise and juice. Spread over top. Bake uncovered 25 to 30 minutes at 350°. Last 5 minutes place cheese on top and allow to melt. Serve with white rice, green or yellow vegetable (carrots, corn, etc.) and a dessert.

James L. Rogers, Retired, and wife Charlotte

MAMA'S CHICKEN & DUMPLINGS

- 1 package chicken breasts
- 3 cans clear chicken broth
- 3 cups flour
- 1½ teaspoons salt
- black pepper
- 1 scant cup shortening

In a large stew pot cook chicken, then remove. Add chicken broth to the stew pot, simmer. In a large bowl sift together flour, salt and pepper. Add shortening and cut in to a mealy stage. Add 1 cup of the boiling chicken broth. Knead in small batches on floured board. Roll, then cut into 1-inch strips. Drop into simmering chicken broth and cook covered about 30 minutes. Add boned chicken.

John Dendy, Retired,
and wife Vineta

CHICKEN 'N' DUMPLINGS

- 4 pounds chicken
- 3 cups sifted flour
- 1 teaspoon salt
- 2 teaspoons baking powder
- ½ cup shortening
- 1 cup milk

Cut chicken into serving pieces and place in large kettle with salted water to cover. Bring to boil, then reduce flame to simmer. Cook until chicken is tender. While chicken is cooking, combine flour, salt and baking powder. With pastry blender, fork or two knives, cut in shortening. Add milk, mixing well. Turn out onto lightly floured board or pastry cloth and knead lightly. Roll out to ⅛-inch thickness. Cut into strips. When chicken is tender, drop strips into kettle. Cover and continue simmering 20 minutes. Makes 8 generous servings.

Captain Jack Dean,
Company D,
and wife Janie

ANN'S CHICKEN SPAGHETTI

- 1¼ cups 2-inch spaghetti pieces
- 1½ cups cooked chicken
- ¼ cup pimientos
- 1 cup chopped green pepper
- ½ cup chopped onion
- 1 cup cream of mushroom soup
- ½ cup chicken broth
- ½ teaspoon salt
- black pepper
- 1¾ cups Cheddar cheese

Cook spaghetti as directed. Combine chicken, pimientos, green pepper and onions. Toss well. Add soup, broth, salt, pepper, 1½ cups cheese and spaghetti. Sprinkle remainder of cheese on top. Bake at 350° for 45 minutes.

Wallace Spillar, Retired,
and wife Ann

CHEESY CHICKEN SPAGHETTI

- 3-4 cooked chicken breasts
- 1 pound pasteurized process cheese spread
- ½ pound Mexican pasteurized process cheese spread
- 1 can cream of chicken soup
- ¾ can milk
- cooked spaghetti

Shred or chop chicken breasts. In large saucepan combine cheeses, soup, milk and chicken. Cook over low heat. Pour over cooked spaghetti. Serve with steamed broccoli and French bread.

Sergeant Kyle Dean,
Company B

MAMA'S TURKEY AND DRESSING

If you buy a frozen turkey, be sure it is well thawed. Put giblets and neck to boil in a saucepan. Rub the turkey inside and out with salt. I melt a stick of butter, dip a piece of cheese cloth doubled in the butter and put over the turkey in the roaster, breast up. From time to time, pour a little water in the roaster. Bake at 325° until the leg will easily pull away from the turkey. (Dressing recipe on page 203.)

John Barron Harris,
Texas Ranger
Association Foundation,
and wife Cheryl

I use a brown and bake bag because it is much easier than the way my mother used to do it.

CHICKEN SPAGHETTI

- 1 (3 to 4 pound) chicken
- 1 (12 ounce) package cut spaghetti
- 2 medium onions, chopped
- 1 large green pepper, chopped
- 1 medium can chopped pimientos
- 1 can mushrooms
- ¼ cup oil
- 4 tablespoons flour
- salt and pepper
- 2 cups milk
- 1 can tomatoes
- ½ cup grated cheese

Stew chicken for 3 to 4 hours. Reserve stock using it to cook the spaghetti. Brown onions, green pepper, pimientos and mushrooms in oil. Add flour, salt and pepper. Cook. Add milk and stir into thick gravy, add tomatoes. Combine mixture with spaghetti, diced chicken and stock. Mix well. Place in greased casserole dish. Cover with cheese. Bake at 350° for 30 minutes.

Captain Walter A. "Bob" Werner, Retired, and wife Jeanne

QUICK CHICKEN ENCHILADAS

- 1 small onion, chopped
- 1 tablespoon oil
- 1 cup cooked, shredded chicken
- ½ cup picante sauce
- ½ teaspoon ground cumin
- 1 cup shredded Monterey Jack cheese
- 4 flour tortillas

Cook onion in oil until tender, but not brown. Stir in chicken, ¼ cup picante sauce and cumin; heat through. Remove from heat; stir in ½ cup cheese. Spoon about ⅓ cup chicken mixture down center of each tortilla; roll up. Place seam side down in 8-inch square baking dish. Spoon remaining picante sauce evenly over enchiladas; sprinkle with remaining cheese. Bake at 350° for 15 minutes or until hot. Top with sliced green onions and sour cream, if desired, and serve with additional picante sauce. This recipe doubles well. Makes 2 servings.

Captain Bob Mitchell, Retired, and wife Jerry

POLLO PIBIL

Cut up a chicken and place the pieces in a bowl. Squeeze lime juice over them until they're just about covered. They should sit about 30 minutes in the juice before being drained. When the chicken pieces are dry enough rub them with olive oil (or any cooking oil) and sprinkle them with paprika. The paprika should be rubbed all over them to give them a pretty red color. The chicken can then be baked or broiled. It depends upon your personal habits about salting the chicken; before cooking or afterward. It won't need much salt. Good served with refried beans, Spanish rice and corn tortillas.

Tom Burks, Curator,
Texas Ranger Museum
And Hall Of Fame,
and wife Laverne

When we got the first proof of this book someone had inadvertently credited Tom Burks with having a wife. I've known him many years and never knew of him being married. I called over at the museum and asked Tom if he had a wife, and his answer was... "No ... I've never had one of my own."

CHERYL'S CORNISH HENS

Wash and prepare 4 whole Cornish hens. Butter hens generously. Salt and pepper outside. Place in center of foil strip in glass baking dish. Prepare 1 box Brown & Wild Rice with seasonings. Cook as per package directions. Sauté ½ cup chopped celery and ½ cup chopped onion in ½ stick butter. Add to rice. Stir in ¼ teaspoon garlic, a dash of thyme, a dash of marjoram, salt and medium ground black pepper to taste. Stuff hens with rice mixture. If there is any left over, sprinkle between hens. Bake at 300° for about 3 hours.

John Barron Harris,
Texas Ranger
Association Foundation,
and wife Cheryl

TURKEY STUFFED PEPPERS

- **4 large bell peppers (red or green)**
- **1 tablespoon oil**
- **1 large onion, chopped**
- **1 clove garlic, finely chopped**
- **1 pound ground turkey**
- **½ teaspoon salt**
- **1½ teaspoons poultry seasoning**
- **¼ cup chopped parsley**
- **½ cup dry breadcrumbs**
- **1 cup barbecue sauce**

Cut peppers in half lengthwise; remove seeds. Red or green peppers may be used. Blanch 5 minutes in large pot of boiling water. Drain cut-side down on paper towels. Heat oil in medium skillet. Add onion and garlic. Cook 30 seconds longer. Set aside. Combine turkey, salt, poultry seasoning, parsley, breadcrumbs and onion mixture in small bowl. Arrange peppers in a 13x9-inch glass baking dish. Spoon turkey mixture into each half. Spoon barbecue sauce over top and bake uncovered in 375° oven for 30 minutes or until meat is cooked. Juices will run clear when pierced with a fork.

Captain Bob Mitchell, Retired, and wife Jerry

GUNN'S FAJITAS

- **beef skirt**
- **Worcestershire sauce**
- **lime juice**
- **garlic salt**
- **lemon pepper**
- **liquid butter**

Make a tray of doubled heavy duty foil. After trimming excess fat and peeling the beef skirt, place in the foil tray. While the skirt is in the foil tray, treat both sides of the meat with generous amounts of the remaining ingredients. Let marinate for 1 to 2 hours. Then place foil tray with meat and all ingredients on grill (pecan wood fire preferred) and cook rather fast (no more than 15 minutes). Remove from grill and save the natural gravy to serve with the meat. Slice the beef skirt and serve with pinto beans, pico de gallo and grated cheese.

Bill Gunn, Retired, and wife Sugar

May substitute onion salt for garlic salt.

RAGIN' CAJUN FRIED TURKEY

Get turkey 2 to 3 days before cooking and thaw. Turkey must be at room temperature. Remove trimmings (inside cavity and under breast skin). Place turkey in large pot. Fill with water until turkey floats. Remove turkey from pot and mark water level. Pour out water and dry the pot. Fill the pot with oil up to the mark. You should have at least 4 inches of pot above this oil to keep hot bubbling oil from spilling over the sides. Drain turkey till dry. Skewer skin flap onto turkey using small skewer like comes with filet mignon. Slit this skin to create drain hole from cavity for oil to drain when removing turkey from pot. Tie legs together with a heavy string long enough to hang outside of the pot. This is what you will use to pull the turkey out of the pot with when done. The oil is very hot and the turkey must drain in order to remain crisp. Fold wing tips inside wings. Season with salt, black pepper, cayenne and garlic powder (use a lot of seasoning). Light fire and heat oil. To determine when oil is hot, I fry a large sliced Irish potato. When it floats, remove it and insert turkey slowly into the oil. (Remember—Long String!) Turkey requires 3 minutes cooking time per pound of turkey. Do not overcook. When done, put the turkey into a roasting pan and allow it to cool for 15 minutes or so. While warm, slice same as an oven-cooked turkey. It should come out golden brown and the skin should be crisp. For gravy pour oil out of pot. Cut 3 large onions and put in pot. Add water and light fire on very low. All of the flavoring that stuck to the bottom of pot will make excellent gravy. Adjust water for thickness desired. This will also help clean the pot.

John Barron Harris,
Texas Ranger
Association Foundation,
and wife Cheryl

This recipe came from my good friend Harold Oubre, from New Iberia, LA. Our friend Harold was an engineer with the old Otis Engineering Co. - a division of Haliburton. He was in charge of their hunting camp where they entertained customers. Harold is an excellent cook both inside with an oven and outside on a campfire. We've eaten lots of good meals with him during the 20 odd years Haliburton had our ranch leased for hunting and recreation.

WEST TEXAS FAJITAS

Take several pounds of skirt steak and slice it into strips about ½-inch to 1-inch wide and several inches long. Put the strips of skirt steak into a deep bowl and pour in enough pineapple juice to completely cover all the meat. (The acid in the juice tenderizes the meat as well as helps cut loose fat from it.) The meat needs to sit in the pineapple juice for at least 24 hours, preferably, 48 hours. Remove meat from juice and rinse under tap water. Place the strips of meat into a second bowl and cover completely with 1 large bottle of Spicy Italian Dressing, 1 cup soy sauce 1 tablespoon garlic salt. Let the meat stand in the seasoning sauce for about 10 to 12 hours. Cook the meat over an open fire (Bar-B-Q Grill) garnishing with onion as it cooks. Remove meat from bowl of seasoning sauce and place directly on the grill. Cook meat until browned and then remove to a tin foil lined bowl so that it stays warm until all meat is cooked. Meat serves best in flour tortillas with guacamole, sour cream, chopped onions and grated cheese. (& hot sauce if you're a real man).

C. J. "Buster" Collins,
Company E

Several years back a prostitute from Austin, Texas, shot her pimp to death in his shower. She contacted her boyfriend and asked him to help her get rid of the body. After the boyfriend got to the house they wrapped the body up in the shower curtain and put it in the boyfriend's trunk. After looking at a Texas map they decided to haul the body to far west Texas hoping to dump the victim where no one would find him.

After traveling a full day they decided to spend the night in Van Horn, Texas. The next morning they purchased a gas can, cotton rope and a shovel. After purchasing gasoline they proceeded to a point approximately seven to eight miles west of Sierra Blanca, Texas. After leaving the interstate on a dirt road they traveled about five more miles where they stopped to dig a shallow grave. They drug the body from the trunk of the car, doused it with gasoline, rolled it over into the grave and set it on fire.

The Border Patrol check point is located just west of Sierra Blanca, Texas, and on that particular day I had stopped to have coffee and visit the border patrolmen, something that I do on a regular basis. A call came in on the radio from a border patrolman who had found a burning body. He reported that there was a strong smell of gasoline around the body.

Within a minute or two after receiving the information the prostitute and her boyfriend drove up to the check point, their gas can still sitting in the back seat. The two subjects were questioned and then were asked if the officers could look into their trunk. The prostitute got out of the car and opened the trunk. Blood was standing in the trunk as well as several pieces of cotton rope similar to the rope the body had been tied up with.

Within two hours both subjects were under arrest for murder and confessions were voluntarily given by both. Rangers in Austin were contacted and provided necessary information which prompted a quick solution to the crime.

I guess there is never anything humorous about someone being murdered, but it was humorous to me to think that two perpetrators took two days to travel more than 500 miles trying to avoid detection only to be under arrest just minutes after dumping the body. This proves that even in a very remote area law enforcement prevails.

I have been in the Texas Rangers for more than twelve years, all of which have been in El Paso. My territory covers El Paso, Hudspeth and Culberson Counties. I graduated DPS recruit school in 1967.

C. J. "Buster" Collins,
Company E

FAJITAS

Tenderize fajita meat. Trim off excess fat. Sprinkle with garlic salt and black pepper; rub in. Marinate with Worcestershire sauce and let set 2 to 3 hours if possible. Prepare sauce for marinating while cooking. Squeeze the juice of one or two limes (depending on amount you use) in to Italian dressing. Add in ½ to a full beer (preferably not a light beer). While cooking fajitas, marinate with dressing, turning about every 3 to 4 minutes and marinating until done. Serve with flour or corn tortillas, pico de gallo, diced chile verde, tomatoes, onion, cilantro, and avocado guacamole (squeeze lime and salt into guacamole).

Sergeant H. Joaquin Jackson,
Company E

This recipe won first place in a fajita cook-off in Midland, Texas a few years ago. Joaquin says that he gave this recipe to a friend who entered it in a cook-off out in Midland, TX. He claimed it as his own and won $300.00 for the recipe

JIM'S FAJITAS

fajita meat
salt & pepper
garlic powder
Liquid Smoke
teriyaki sauce

Remove fat and waste from meat, as much as possible. Cut meat into hand size pieces and tenderize. Add salt, pepper and garlic powder the meat on both sides. Place in marinating pan and sprinkle with Liquid Smoke and teriyaki sauce on both sides. Allow to marinate overnight for best results. Place on barbecue pit or grill and cook until done. This takes just a few minutes. Personally, I like the meat a little crisp around the edges.

Jim Peters, Retired,
and wife Lydia

This recipe won first place in the South Texas Fajita Cook-Off. A panel of five judges voted in favor 4 to 1. The dissenting judge (the Corpus Christi Chief of Police's secretary) said that she could not taste the meat for the seasoning, therefore, she did not give me a first place vote.

RAY'S BBQ BRISKET

- seasoned salt
- black pepper
- ground red pepper
- brisket
- sliced onions
- sliced lemons
- Italian dressing

Make a rub with the seasoned salt, black pepper and red pepper. Apply liberally to the brisket. Put on top of ice in cooler. Top brisket with onions and lemons, top with more ice. Marinate overnight. Smoke on outdoor pit. Use Italian dressing as a mop.

Sergeant Ray Nutt, Company F

STEAK WITH WHISKEY SAUCE

- 1 large 2-inch thick sirloin steak
- 1 tablespoon coarsely crushed black peppercorns
- 2-3 cloves garlic, minced
- ½ teaspoon coarse rock salt
- ¼ pound butter
- 2 tablespoon chopped onion
- 1 clove garlic, minced
- 2 tablespoons whiskey
- 1 tablespoon Worcestershire sauce
- ½ teaspoon dry mustard
- dash hot pepper sauce

Trim excess fat from steak. Press crushed peppercorns and garlic into both sides of steak and let stand at room temperature for one hour. Heat a heavy black iron skillet over high heat. Grease the bottom of the hot skillet with a piece of fat that you trimmed off the steak. Toss in about half of the salt. Sear the steak or steaks quickly on one side, then lift out. Add remaining salt to the skillet, turn the steak and sear on the other side. Reduce the heat to medium and cook the steaks as desired. Remove to a warm platter. Pour off any fat from cooking the steak. Melt butter in the same skillet over low heat; add onion and garlic and cook slowly until soft. Add remaining ingredients and simmer for a minute or two. Pour over steaks and serve.

**Captain Jack Dean,
Company D,
and wife Janie**

RANGER SWISS STEAK

- 2 pounds boneless beef round steak
- 1/4 cup flour
- 1 teaspoon salt
- 1/4 teaspoon black pepper
- 1 cup thinly sliced celery
- 1 medium thinly sliced onion
- 1 cup thinly sliced green pepper
- 1 can tomato soup
- 2/3 cup water
- 1 tablespoon Worcestershire sauce

Trim round steak; pound well. Cut into 6 or 8 pieces. Mix flour, salt and pepper. Coat beef with flour mixture and beat again. Place meat in frying pan and brown on both sides. Sauté celery, onion and green pepper. Mix with remaining ingredients. Pour over beef. Simmer until beef is tender; 40 to 50 minutes in microwave; 1 to 1½ hours on range or in electric skillet. Meat should be tender enough to cut with a fork.

Sergeant W. R. "Bill" Gerth,
Company C,
and wife Dixie

"WE'LL GET PLENTY FOR SUPPER"

This is one old retired Ranger who can heat water and sometimes burn it. I was always smart enough to stay close to Bill Gunn and Max Womack when it was time to prepare a meal. Some Rangers just excel in other areas. Red Arnold and I would go out and kill whatever needed killing and depend on others to cook it or burn it. Cooking just don't seem to fit this old retired Ranger. Now when Red Arnold, Bob Mitchell and I thought something needed killing we would try and do the job if it was just to fill the cook's pot. Plenty of stories about Red will most likely surface for your book. One that stands out in my mind was a trip to Lake of the Pines with Red and Jim Day. We were about to embark on a little fishing one afternoon and a friend of mine was coming in. He offered us a nice string of fish and Red declined. Later that night we had dinner at a cafe in Lone Star. Red's famous last words to my friend were "We'll catch plenty for supper."

Glenn Elliott, Retired

CABBAGE ROLLS À LA CAJUN

- 1 pound pork ground meat
- 1 pound lean ground beef
- ½ cup chopped onions
- ½ cup chopped bell pepper
- 1 tablespoon salt
- 1 tablespoon black pepper
- ¾ cup long grain white rice, raw
- 1 can Rotel tomatoes, diced with chillies
- 1 (8 ounce) can tomato sauce
- 1 teaspoon red cayenne pepper

Combine all above in large bowl. Mix well with hands. Very gooey. Put to boil two large cabbage heads, well cored in center. Cook for 45 minutes to soften leaves. Remove from hot water. Separate large leaves - cut out in v-shape 1-inch. Into center of large leaf, using large spoon, put mixture and roll into leaf, careful to fold ends to contain mixture. Into a large pot, with metal rack on bottom, place each roll on rack, stack them all around. Note: Do not roll tight! They will swell. When all are stacked pour on top 1 can diced Rotel tomatoes, 1 can tomato sauce, plus 2 cups water, and begin to cook. It must boil to cook meat and rice. Do not boil hard, very slow - gurgling - for 2 hours. If it seems dry add water. After 2 hours, try one - eat all of it - umm, umm!

John Barron Harris,
Texas Ranger
Association Foundation,
and wife Cheryl

Another recipe from my good friend and camp cook Harold Oubre, New Iberia, La.

MAGIC EYE OF ROUND

4½ pound beef eye of round roast
8 ounces brown mustard
3-4 cups kosher salt

Cover all sides and ends of the roast with brown mustard, using entire amount. Place kosher salt on a plate; roll the roast in it, covering it completely (the salt coating should be thick with no meat or mustard visible.) Place the roast on a rack in a roasting pan. Bake in a 475° to 500° oven for 10 to 12 minutes per pound for rare, 12 to 15 minutes per pound for medium and 15 to 20 minutes per pound for well done. When the roast is cooked to the desired degree of doneness, crack the surface with a knife and remove the outer casing of salt and mustard. Have pan available to hold the encased juices. Carve the roast in thin slices. Serve meat juices in a gravy boat.

Captain Jack Dean,
Company D,
and wife Janie

Handle roast with tongs at all times. A fork or knife might pierce the salt casing. A 4½ pound roast will take approximately 40 minutes total cooking time for medium doneness.

BARBECUE PORK RIBS

pork ribs
Worcestershire sauce
garlic salt
coarse ground black pepper
paprika
chili powder

Put ribs in container and sprinkle generously with Worcestershire sauce, then rub ribs with dry ingredients and marinate refrigerated overnight. Place ribs on grill with meat side up and do not turn over.

Bill Gunn, Retired,
and wife Sugar

PEDERNALES PORK

- 2 pounds pork tenderloins
- 6 medium chopped onions
- ½ cup oil
- 1 teaspoon salt
- 1 teaspoon paprika
- ¾ teaspoon black pepper
- ¼ teaspoon crushed red chilies
- 1-2 sliced sweet red peppers

Cut meat into julienne strips. Sauté onions in ¼ cup oil in skillet for 2 to 3 minutes. Stir in spices and chilies. Place on low heat to keep warm. In separate skillet, brown pork in remaining ¼ cup oil. Cook over medium heat 15 to 20 minutes. Top meat with pepper pieces. Cover and simmer 5 minutes. Stir in onion mixture. Garnish with 1-inch cubes of feta cheese, if desired. Serves 8.

Sergeant L. R. "Rocky" Wardlow,
Headquarters Company

RANCH PORK LOIN

- 4-6 pounds pork loin; washed and trimmed
- whole cloves
- 1 large onion; whole and cleaned
- 1 bay leaf
- 3-4 cans beer; room temperature
- 2 teaspoons salt
- 1 teaspoon black pepper
- 3 eggs, beaten
- 2 cups Italian Style breadcrumbs

Place pork loin in a large pan. Stick cloves all around sides of onion. Place in middle of pan containing loin. Add bay leaf, beer, salt and pepper. Cover and simmer over low heat for 2 hours. Drain, reserving stock. Cool 20 to 30 minutes or longer. Preheat oven to 400°. Roll loin in beaten eggs, then in breadcrumbs. Bake until browned. Baste with reserved stock while cooking. Thicken remaining stock with flour for a great sauce to serve over sliced medallions.

John Barron Harris,
Texas Ranger
Association Foundation,
and wife Cheryl

COUNTRY PEPPERS

8 large whole bell peppers
1 pound ground beef
1 pound pork sausage
½ cup onion
1½ cups cooked rice
1 (16 ounce) jar pasteurized processed cheese spread
½ cup chopped tomatoes
ketchup

Remove tops and seeds from peppers. Par boil 5 minutes. Drain on paper towels. Brown meat and drain. Add chopped onion. Cover and cook on until tender. Stir in rice, cheese and tomatoes. Fill pepper. Top with ketchup. Place in baking dish with a little water and cover. Bake at 350° for 40 minutes.

6 servings

John Barron Harris,
Texas Ranger
Association Foundation,
and wife Cheryl

CHICKEN FRIED HAM

Take a fresh ham and have it sliced into ½-inch steaks. Cut the steaks into 4 cutlets and tenderize them with a steak tenderizing machine or a mallet. Salt and pepper the cutlets. Batter them in flour. (Dip the cutlets in milk before flouring them if you desire.) Heat cooking oil in a skillet. Fry the cutlets in the oil using a covered skillet until they are done. Usually one turning of the cutlets is plenty if the oil is hot enough. This dish tastes like veal cutlets.

Sergeant John Aycock,
Company F,
and wife Estelle

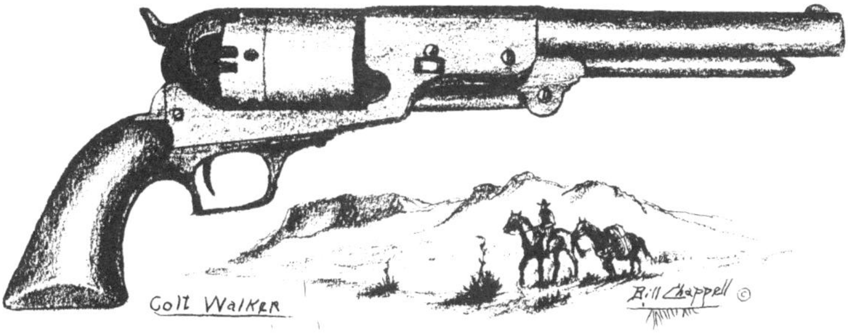

PEDERNALES RIVER CHILI

- 4 pounds chili meat
- 1 large onion, chopped
- 2 cloves minced garlic
- 1 teaspoon ground oregano
- 1 teaspoon cumin seed
- 2 tablespoons chili powder
- salt
- 2 cans tomatoes and green chilies
- 2-6 dashes hot pepper sauce
- 2 cups hot water

Sear meat, onions and garlic in large, heavy boiler or skillet until lightly browned. Add seasonings, tomatoes, pepper sauce and water. Bring to a boil. Lower heat. Simmer about 1 hour. As chili cooks, skim off fat.

Serves 10.

Captain Jack Dean,
Company D,
and wife Janie

NORTH TEXAS RED CHILI

- 2½ pounds diced, boneless chuck roast
- 1 tablespoon melted shortening
- 4 cups water
- ¼ cup diced onion
- 1 teaspoon garlic powder
- 1 teaspoon salt
- ½ teaspoon red pepper
- 4 whole jalapeño peppers
- 6 tablespoons chili powder
- 4 teaspoons ground cumin
- ½ teaspoon oregano
- ⅛ teaspoon ground bay leaf
- 2 cubes beef bouillon
- 8 ounces tomato sauce

Brown meat in shortening in Dutch oven. Add water, onion, garlic powder, salt, ¼ teaspoon red pepper, and jalapeño peppers. Bring to a boil and simmer, uncovered for 1 hour. Add water as needed to keep liquid ½ inch above meat throughout cooking procedure. Remove jalapeños and strain liquid from peppers. Add pepper liquid, 3 tablespoons chili powder, 2 teaspoons cumin, ¼ teaspoon oregano, bay leaf, bouillon cubes and tomato sauce. Stir well. Simmer, uncovered, 1 hour and 45 minutes. Add remaining chili powder, cumin and red pepper. Simmer about 15 minutes. Yield: 6½ cups.

Sergeant Jim Gillespie,
Company C

MAMA'S CHILI

I make my own chili, and I think this is a real good recipe.

4 pounds ground meat
½ pound ground suet (save the trimmings off your steaks)
2 tablespoons salt
1 teaspoon garlic salt
2 large onions
2 tablespoons paprika
2 teaspoons chili pepper
1 teaspoon red pepper
6 heaping tablespoons Chili Blend (I like it better than chili powder)
2 tablespoons sugar
1 #2 can tomato juice

Combine all of the ingredients. Add water if necessary. Sometimes I add half a bottle of ketchup. Let it cook for several hours. I usually thicken it with about 2 tablespoons flour and enough water to make a paste. Add slowly, stirring all the while. This is nice to have in the freezer to eat on cold nights. Try it - I think you will like it. If you don't have your own meat, have them grind you 3 pounds of chili meat at the market and buy 1 pound of hamburger and ½ pound of suet.

John Barron Harris,
Texas Ranger
Association Foundation,
and wife Cheryl

Before I graduated from high school in 1946, I bought a penny arcade and confectionery on Grant Avenue, the main street at the time, in Odessa, Texas. My mother and dad did not know I was going into business, but I had $500 to pay down and the people I bought it from didn't know how old I was. Mama worked at the Ector County Clerk's Office but at night she made pecan pies and chili for me to sell. I sold thousands of bowls of this chili. I make mine a little different now, but this helped make my payments in the old days.

TEXAS JAILBREAK CHILI

- 2 pounds ground beef
- 1 chopped green pepper
- 2 cloves garlic, minced
- 2-3 tablespoons chili powder
- 1 tablespoon ground cumin
- 2 teaspoons salt
- 1 teaspoon coriander
- 12 ounces beer or water
- 1 (6 ounce) can tomato paste

Crumble beef into a dishwasher safe plastic colander. Set over a 3-quart round casserole. Sprinkle bell pepper and garlic on top. Microwave on high 8 to 10 minutes, stirring midway through cooking. Discard grease from casserole and transfer meat mixture into it. Add chili powder, cumin, salt and coriander; stir well. Add beer and tomato paste, stir. Microwave on high 10 minutes stirring midway through cooking. Freezes well. Makes 6 servings.

John Barron Harris,
Texas Ranger
Association Foundation,
and wife Cheryl

CAMP FIRE FISH

Take fish filets and place on foil. Sprinkle with lemon juice, lemon pepper, sliced onions and butter. Seal foil around fish air tight. Cook maybe 30 minutes over coals.

Johnny Harris

This recipe was given to us by our old friends, Dale and Brandon Sommerfeld. Dale and Brandon come to our ranch to cook "for the boys" and always catch a few fish while they are BBQ'ing. They use this method to cook mouth-watering fish on the pit.

SALMON PATTIES

- 1 can pink salmon
- 1 egg
- 1/3 cup minced onion
- 1/2 cup flour
- 1 1/2 teaspoons baking powder

Save 2 tablespoons juice from salmon. Put baking powder in juice and add to other ingredients. Make into patties and fry till brown.

Sgt. Billy Peterson, Company C
and wife Barbara

COLORADO RIVER CATFISH

2 (6-8 ounce) catfish fillets
1 cup cornmeal
1 tablespoon garlic salt
1 tablespoon paprika
1 teaspoon black pepper
pinch ground cloves
flour
eggwash
3 tablespoons flour
½ cup bacon drippings
1½ cups milk
1 tablespoon chicken bouillon
dash Worcestershire sauce
salt & pepper

Cut each fillet into 3 or 4 pieces. Mix together cornmeal, garlic salt, paprika, pepper and cloves for breading mixture. Dredge each piece of catfish in flour, then eggwash, coating well. Next dredge in breading mixture coating all sides well. Deep-fry in 360° degree oil (I prefer peanut oil) for 2 to 3 minutes until golden brown. For gravy, whisk flour into bacon drippings over medium heat until smooth. Add milk while you continue to whisk the mixture until it is mixed in and gravy is smooth. Add bouillon, stir until dissolved. Stir in Worcestershire, salt and pepper. Serve immediately over catfish.

Sergeant L. R. "Rocky" Wardlow,
Headquarters Company

CRAWFISH ÉTOUFÉE

1 medium chopped onion
½ cup chopped green onions
1 chopped bell pepper
2 tablespoons butter
1 pound peeled crawfish
1 can golden mushroom soup
cayenne pepper
salt & pepper

Sauté onions and pepper in butter over high heat, stirring constantly until they are almost cooked down. Add crawfish and soup. Stir all together for a few additional minutes. Reduce heat to low setting, cover and let simmer approximately 30 minutes, stirring occasionally. Season to taste. Serve hot over a bed of rice. Makes approximately 4 servings.

Sergeant L. C. Wilson,
Company A

The crawfish is seasonal and can be purchased already peeled and packaged. You can keep it in a freezer and thaw when ready to cook. Being more than half of Cajun descent myself, this recipe is a tasty favorite of mine.

SOUTH TEXAS SHRIMP

shrimp
melted butter or margarine
salt & pepper
medium picante sauce

Peel and devein shrimp. Make a tray from heavy duty foil that will fit on grill of a barbecue pit. Curl up the edges of the foil so it will hold the juices. Put plenty of butter in bottom of tray (approximately ¼-inch deep). Salt and pepper the shrimp and place one layer in the tray. Pour picante sauce over the shrimp and cook slowly until the shrimp are done. Don't overcook or they will be tough. You can sample as they cook, but save some for others.

**Jim Peters, Retired,
and wife Lydia**

LAURA'S MEXICAN CASSEROLE

2 pounds ground beef
1 medium chopped onion
1 teaspoon chili powder
½ teaspoon garlic powder
2 cans cream of mushroom soup
1 can diced tomatoes and green chilies
3 tablespoons medium picante sauce
flour tortillas
grated cheese

Brown meat, drain. Add onion, chili powder and garlic powder. Cook until onions are clear. Mix in soup, tomatoes and green chilies and picante sauce. Quarter tortillas and place a layer in bottom of casserole dish, overlapping. Add layer of meat mixture and a layer of cheese. Continue layers as needed ending with a layer of cheese on top. Place in 350° oven and bake for 1 hour.

**Capt. James Wright, Retired,
and wife Laura**

QUICK MEXICAN CASSEROLE

- 1 can tamales
- 1 can refried beans
- 1 can corn
- 1 can chili
- 1½ cups shredded cheese

Preheat oven to 350°. Shuck tamales. Place all ingredients layered as written in greased casserole dish. Heat until bubbling and cheese is melted. Serve with crackers or tortillas.

**Bill Gunn, Retired,
and wife Sugar**

MEXICAN CASSEROLE

- 1 pound ground beef
- 1 can cream of mushroom soup
- 1 can cream of chicken soup
- 1 can enchilada sauce
- 1 cup milk
- 12 corn tortillas
- grated cheese

Brown meat and drain. Add next 4 ingredients and heat till bubbly. Place six tortillas in bottom of 13x9-inch baking dish. Spoon half of meat mixture on top. Sprinkle with grated cheese. Add remaining tortillas. Top with remaining meat mixture and top with more cheese. Heat through and serve.

**Sergeant Danny Rhea,
Company B,
and wife Sue**

BEEF NACHO CASSEROLE

- 1 pound ground beef
- ½ cup chopped onions
- 1 (12 ounce) jar chunky salsa
- 1 can whole kernel corn
- ¾ cup Miracle Whip salad dressing
- 1 tablespoon chili powder
- 2 cups crushed tortilla chips
- 2 cups shredded colby or Monterey Jack

Heat oven to 350°. Brown meat and onions, drain. Stir in salsa, corn, Miracle Whip and chili powder. Layer half of meat mixture, chips and cheese in 2-quart casserole. Repeat layers. Bake 20 minutes or until heated. Top with shredded lettuce and chopped tomatoes. Makes 6 servings.

**Bill Gunn, Retired,
and wife Sugar**

LOWFAT MEXICAN CASSEROLE

- 1 pound ground turkey
- 1 small chopped onion
- 1 clove minced garlic
- 1 tablespoon vinegar
- 2 teaspoon chili powder
- 1½ teaspoons crushed oregano
- ½ teaspoon cumin
- pinch ground red pepper
- ½ cup water
- 15 ounces drained kidney beans
- 16 ounces picante sauce
- 6 6-inch corn tortillas
- ¾ cup reduced fat Cheddar cheese

Cook turkey, onion and garlic in large skillet. Drain off fat. Add vinegar, chili powder, oregano, cumin, red pepper and water. Cook 1 minute and stir in beans. Remove from heat. In a 13x9-inch pan place about 2 tablespoons picante. Cut tortillas in 1-inch strips. Place about ½ of tortilla strips on top of picante. Place half of the turkey mixture on top of strips and then top with ½ of remaining picante. Repeat layers. Cover with grated cheese. Use foil or lid to cover and bake in a preheated 325° oven for 30 minutes. Can uncover and bake another 5 to 10 minutes if desired. 286 calories, 11 grams fat.

**Captain Dan North, Retired,
and wife Nancy**

TEX-MEX TACO PIE

- 1 pound ground beef
- ½ cup chopped onion
- 1 envelope taco seasoning
- 4 ounces chopped green chilies
- ¾ cup biscuit mix
- 1¼ cups milk
- 3 eggs
- 2 sliced tomatoes
- 1 cup shredded cheese

Heat oven to 400°. Grease a 10-inch pie plate. In skillet, sauté beef and onions. Drain off fat. Stir in taco seasoning. Spread meat mixture into pie pan and top with drained green chilies. In separate bowl, beat biscuit mix, milk and eggs until smooth. Pour over meat layer and bake 25 minutes. Top pie with tomato slices, then cheese and return to oven for another 10 minutes. When pie is done, knife inserted into center will emerge clean.

**Sergeant Jim Gillespie,
Company C**

SPANISH CASSEROLE

- 2 tablespoons chopped onion
- 2 tablespoons butter
- 1 can cream of mushroom soup
- 1 can cream of chicken soup
- 1 can tomatoes and green chilies
- 2 cups cooked, boned chicken
- tortilla chips
- grated cheese

Sauté onions in butter. Add soup, tomatoes and green chilies and chicken. Bring to a boil. Place chips in casserole dish. Top with meat mixture, then cheese. Bake in oven long enough to melt cheese.

Sergeant Coy L. Smith, Company D, and wife Pat

This recipe is submitted in memory of Claudine Smith, mother of Coy L. Smith, Sergeant, Texas Rangers Company "D", stationed in Uvalde. Mrs. Smith passed away on July 4, 1986 only six months before Coy was promoted to 'Texas Ranger'. Prior to her death, Mrs. Smith related stories about her childhood and the fact that her Uncle was a Texas Ranger and stationed near Livingston, Texas. This recipe which was prepared often by Mrs. Smith has a South Texas flair which is common to where we now reside.

GREEN ENCHILADAS

- 16 ounces Monterey Jack cheese
- 1 large carton sour cream
- 1 can chopped green chilies
- 1 pound ground beef
- 1 small chopped onion
- 12 corn tortillas
- ½ pound grated longhorn cheese

Cut Monterey Jack cheese into cubes and mix with sour cream. Add green chilies. Heat over low heat until cheese melts. Brown meat and onion. Soften tortillas in hot oil. Put 2 tablespoons meat in each tortilla and roll up. Place rolled up tortillas in 9x13-inch (or larger) pan. Pour sour cream mixture over enchiladas. Layer longhorn cheese on top. Bake 20 minutes at 350°.

Clayton Mckinney, Retired

Caution-these are traffic stoppers. I recommend you hide and eat the first batch yourself!

HAMBURGER FIESTA

1 pound ground beef
1 medium chopped onion
1 medium chopped bell pepper
½ cup water
4-6 cups cooked or oven beans

Place all ingredients in skillet on medium heat. Cook until done and then add beans. Season to taste with the following: garlic salt, black pepper, paprika and chili powder. Stir frequently

Bill Gunn, Retired,
and wife Sugar

Two Rangers were on assignment in South Texas. It was late when they pitched camp and soon to be dark. They were both hungry. One of the men pulled out his lunch and started to eat. The other Ranger had nothing to eat and he asked for some of the food. The Ranger with the food said, "Oh, I just brought this for my own use." Later on, about dark, the mosquitoes boiled up out of the bottom and the Ranger that had nothing to eat pulled out some insect repellant and began to spray it on. The other Ranger asked to use some of it. The Ranger with the spray said to him, "Oh, I couldn't do that, I just brought it along for my own use."

Bill Gunn, Retired

SCRAMBLED BRAINS

½ pound brains
1½ teaspoons vinegar
½ teaspoon salt
2 tablespoons butter
4 beaten eggs
1 tablespoon milk
¼ teaspoon salt

Cover brains with cold water. Add vinegar and soak 30 minutes, drain. Remove loose fatty membrane. Cover brains with water, add ½ teaspoon salt. Simmer 20 to 30 minutes. Drain and chill in cold water. Finely chop brains, brown in butter. Combine eggs, milk and ¼ teaspoon salt. Add to brains. Scramble. Serves 4.

Gaines de Graffenried,
Late Curator Texas Ranger
Museum And Hall Of Fame,
and wife Ola

"My father loved this old recipe for breakfast and sometimes after a long day of trading for a late night supper." Submitted by his son, Tommy de Graffenried.

BREAKFAST TACOS

- 3 slices bacon
- 2 small cubed potatoes
- 2 eggs
- salt & pepper
- flour tortillas

Fry bacon, cut in small pieces and set aside. Fry potatoes in drippings. Drain well when done. Beat eggs with salt and pepper. Combine bacon and potatoes in skillet. Pour eggs over them. Remove and serve when eggs are done. Wrap in flour tortillas for breakfast tacos.

Toliver H. Dawson, Retired

HAM & CHEESE BRUNCH PUFF

- 2 cups ground ham
- 2 cups grated Swiss cheese
- ½ cup mayonnaise
- 1 teaspoon Dijon mustard
- 12 slices bread
- 6 eggs
- 2 cups milk
- ¼ teaspoon hot pepper sauce
- ½ teaspoon salt
- ½ teaspoon black pepper

Stir together ham, cheese, mayonnaise and mustard. Spread on 6 slices of toasted bread. Top with remaining slices of bread to make 6 sandwiches. Cut diagonally into quarters. Stand sandwich quarters on edge, crust sides down, in 9x13-inch baking pan. Combine eggs, milk, pepper sauce, salt and pepper and pour over sandwiches. Mixture may not completely cover sandwiches; do not worry if it doesn't. Cover and chill in refrigerator overnight or a minimum of 4 hours. Bake uncovered in preheated 325° oven until custard is set, about 30 to 40 minutes.

Captain Jack Dean,
Company D,
and wife Janie

EGGS, CHILIES & CHEESE

- 2 small cans chopped green chilies
- 8 eggs
- baking powder
- ½ pound grated Monterey Jack cheese
- 1 pound cooked, drained sausage

Put row of chilies in casserole. Beat eggs with a little milk and pinch of baking powder. Place layer of cheese over the green chilies, then pour eggs over the top. Crumble sausage and sprinkle over all. Bake 300° for 45 minutes to 1 hour.

Sgt. Jesse Priest, Retired

DEER CAMP BREAKFAST

- 2 pounds sausage (any kind: pork venison, etc.)
- 4 dozen well-beaten eggs
- 2 finely chopped jalapeño peppers
- flour tortillas

In a huge cast iron skillet, brown the sausage, then add the eggs. Mix well. Stir in the jalapeños, no large pieces, please. Cook until done. The green adds a nice color to the dish and gives it somewhat of a kick. Spoon onto a warm flour tortilla and roll like a cigar, folding the end up to avoid leakage.

Lieutenant Robert C. Favor, Retired

This particular recipe is a winner in a mule deer camp in far west Texas where I have been guiding and cooking breakfast the past several years.

One year an out of state hunter brought his lady friend to the deer camp. Apparently she was accustomed to better accommodations than camp afforded. After four days her state of mind, not to mention her attitude, was a bit on edge when I set this sumptuous meal before her. She spied the small green bits of jalapeños and inquired as to what it was. I explained that it was jalapeños for flavor. She jumped up and said "My God, they even put peppers in their breakfasts!" She turned to her companion and advised him she would be taking her breakfast in Pecos, with or without him. The jalapeños did the trick because she never showed up again.

Lieutenant Robert C. Favor, Retired

SWEET-AND-SOUR MEATBALLS

- 1 pound ground beef
- 1 small onion
- 2½ cups breadcrumbs
- salt & pepper
- 1 cup apricot preserves
- 2 cups barbecue sauce

Combine meat, onion, breadcrumbs, salt and pepper. Make meatballs and brown in small amount of cooking oil. Mix preserves and sauce. Pour over meatballs. Bake at 350° for 30 minutes.

Sergeant Milton Wright,
Company A,
and wife Marian

SOUPY RANGER MEATBALLS

- 2 slices bread
- 1 pound lean ground beef
- ¼ cup chopped onion
- ¼ cup chopped bell pepper
- 1 beaten egg
- 1½ tablespoons soy sauce
- 1 teaspoon garlic powder
- ½ teaspoon black pepper
- ½ teaspoon salt
- 1 teaspoon oil
- 1 can beef broth
- 1 can tomato sauce
- 2 cups water
- 6 ounces small, shell macaroni

Tear bread slices in small pieces. Combine meat, onion, bell pepper, egg, soy sauce, garlic powder, pepper and salt. Form into 12 to 15 balls. Heat oil in a large, deep skillet. Brown the meatballs. Add beef broth, tomato sauce and water. Let simmer for 5 minutes. Add macaroni and simmer until the shells are soft. Add water for the desired soupy consistency. Season with garlic powder, black pepper and salt to your taste. Excellent in cold weather to warm you up.

Ramiro "Ray" Martinez, Retired

QUICK SUNDAY MEAL

- 2 cans cream of chicken soup
- 1 can water
- 2 pounds stew meat

Combine soup and water. Add meat. Season with onions and Accent. Bake at 325° for 3 hours uncovered. Serve over cooked rice or noodles and carrots if desired.

Captain Carl Weathers,
Company C,
and wife Mickey

This recipe comes from my sister-in-law, Marjorie Sheffield.

LOW-CALORIE CASSEROLE

- 1 small head cabbage
- 1 pound lean ground beef
- 1 small onion, chopped
- ½ cup raw rice
- 1 can condensed tomato soup
- 1 small can tomato sauce
- 1½ cans water

Chop cabbage and place in greased baking dish. Sauté meat and onion. Stir in rice. Pour on top of cabbage. Mix soup, tomato sauce, and water. Pour over entire casserole. Cover and bake at 350° for 1 hour. Add more water if casserole seems too dry.

**Sergeant Kyle Dean,
Company B**

30 MINUTE CASSEROLE

- 1 package stuffing mix
- 2½ cups cooked, diced chicken
- 1 small can sliced water chestnuts
- 1 stick melted butter
- 1⅓ cups chicken broth
- 1 cup sour cream
- 1 can cream of chicken soup

Spray a 9x12-inch casserole with Pam. Prepare stuffing mix according to package directions. Spread stuffing in bottom. Top with cooked chicken and sliced water chestnuts. Combine and blend melted butter, chicken broth, sour cream and soup. Pour over chicken and stuffing. Bake uncovered at 350° for 30 minutes.

**Bobby Poynter, Retired,
and wife Jo**

GLORIFIED GROUND BEEF

- 1 pound lean ground beef
- 3 medium onions, chopped
- 1 large diced bell pepper
- 1 teaspoon salt
- ½ teaspoon black pepper
- ½ teaspoon sugar
- ¼ teaspoon oregano
- 3 cloves garlic
- 1 can chili beans
- 1 can corn

In heavy skillet, brown meat, onions and pepper. Add spices, beans and corn. Simmer a few minutes. Serve while hot.

**Sergeant Danny Rhea,
Company B,
and wife Sue**

WARD'S CRESCENT LASAGNA

- ½ pound sausage
- ½ pound ground beef
- ¾ cup chopped onion
- ½ clove garlic, minced
- 1 tablespoon parsley flakes
- ½ teaspoon basil leaf
- ½ teaspoon leaf oregano
- ½ teaspoon salt
- dash coarse ground pepper
- 1 (6 ounce) can tomato paste
- 1 cup creamed cottage cheese
- 1 egg
- ¼ cup grated Parmesan cheese
- 2 cans refrigerated crescent rolls
- 2 slices (7x4-inch) mozzarella cheese
- 1 tablespoon milk
- 1 tablespoon sesame seed

Preheat oven to 375°. In a large skillet, brown meat and drain. Add onion, garlic, parsley, seasonings and tomato paste. Simmer uncovered for 5 minutes. Combine cottage cheese, egg and Parmesan in a small bowl. Unroll crescent dough and separate into 8 rectangles. On greased cookie sheet, place dough rectangles together overlapping edges (about 15x13-inch rectangle). Press edges to seal. Spread half of meat mixture lengthwise down center of dough. Top meat with cheese mixture. Spoon remaining meat over top forming 3 layers. Place mozzarella slices over top. Fold 13-inch ends of dough rectangle over filling 1 inch. Pull long sides of dough rectangle over filling, being careful to overlap edges. Pinch overlapped edges to seal. Brush with milk and sprinkle with sesame seed. Bake for 20 to 25 minutes or until deep golden brown. Serve with a green salad.

Cheryl Harris,
Texas Ranger
Association Foundation

This recipe belonged to my mother, Pauline Ward Taylor. She made this for all of the kids on the basketball team and any extra strays that happened to show up when I was a teenager. It was always a hit.

HEADQUARTERS HASH

1 pound ground beef
3 large sliced onions
1 large chopped green pepper
1 pound can tomatoes
½ cup uncooked rice
2 teaspoons chili powder
2 teaspoons salt
⅛ teaspoon pepper

Heat oven to 350°. In large skillet cook and stir ground beef. Drain fat and add onions and green peppers. Cook and stir until onion is tender. Stir in tomatoes, rice, chili powder, salt and pepper. Heat through and pour into ungreased 2-quart casserole dish. Cover and bake 1 hour.

Sergeant L. R. "Rocky" Wardlow,
Headquarters Company

This is a favorite of the Junior Rangers in Headquarters Company.

KING RANCH CASSEROLE

1 chicken
1 can cream of mushroom soup
1 can cream of chicken soup
1 can tomatoes and green chilies
½ can chicken broth
1 dozen corn tortillas
1 chopped onion
2 cups grated cheese

Cook chicken in small amount of water, lightly salted, until tender. Bone and cut into pieces. For sauce blend soup, tomatoes and green chilies and chicken broth. Set aside. Into a 2½-quart greased casserole, place a layer of chicken. Cut tortillas into pieces and layer on top of chicken. Layer onion, ½ of the cheese, and ½ of the sauce mixture. Repeat the layers, ending with grated cheese. Bake uncovered for 1 hour at 350°. Yield: 8 servings.

Captain Jack Dean,
Company D,
and wife Janie

COWBOY CASSEROLE

2 pounds ground beef
1 medium onion, chopped
1 teaspoon chili powder
salt & pepper
1 can cream of mushroom soup
1 small can chopped green chilies
1 can tomatoes and green chilies
1 small can tomatoes
1 medium package tortilla chips
1 pound longhorn cheese, grated

Brown ground beef with onion. Season with chili powder, salt and pepper. Add soup, chilies and tomatoes. Stir and bring to boil. Simmer over medium heat 10 to 15 minutes. Line baking pan with chips. Pour mixture over them and top with cheese. Heat in oven at 325° for 15 minutes.

Sergeant Jim Gillespie, Company C

QUICHE

2 beaten eggs
2 cups milk
½ teaspoon salt
½ cup chopped onion
1 cup chopped ham
½ cup grated cheese
1 9-inch pie shell

Chicken may be substituted for ham.

Mix all ingredients together. Pour into shell and bake at 350° until golden brown and knife comes out clean when pierced into center. Sprinkle with small amount of cheese. Yield: 6 servings.

Anonymous Texas Ranger

ITALIAN EASTER PIE

4 beaten eggs
¼ cup milk
½ cup moist, diced pepperoni
½ cup moist, diced salami
½ pound grated mozzarella cheese
¼ teaspoon black pepper
½ teaspoon basil
½ teaspoon oregano
1 unbaked pie shell

Beat eggs and milk together. Add all other ingredients and mix well. Pour into pie shell and bake at 425° for 35 to 40 minutes.

Buzz Dulick, Texas Ranger Association Foundation, and wife Judy

ALVA'S MEATLOAF

1 pound ground beef
½ pound sausage
1 slightly beaten egg
1 cup canned tomatoes
1 cup fine breadcrumbs
1 teaspoon salt
⅛ teaspoon pepper
1 chopped onion
1 cup chopped celery
1 teaspoon Worcestershire sauce
½ cup milk

Combine all ingredients and bake at 350° for 1 to 1½ hours.

Alva Stem, Retired Director of Parks and Recreation Department City of Waco, and wife Helen, Foundation Members

MEAT LOAF

1½ pounds ground beef
1 slightly beaten egg
1 cup breadcrumbs
1 medium onion, chopped
1 can tomato sauce
¼ teaspoon black pepper
1½ teaspoons salt
1 cup water
2 tablespoons brown sugar
2 tablespoons prepared mustard
2 tablespoons vinegar

Mix meat, egg, breadcrumbs, onion, ½ can tomato sauce, pepper and salt. Form into a loaf. Put it in oven while you make a basting sauce, using the remaining tomato sauce, water, brown sugar, mustard and vinegar. Pour over loaf and baste occasionally. Cook 1¼ hours at 350°.

Bill Nelson, Retired, and wife Joyce

BBQ CUPS

1 pound ground beef
½ cup BBQ sauce
1 tablespoon minced onion
1½ tablespoons brown sugar
1 can biscuits
¾ cup shredded Cheddar cheese

Brown meat, stir in sauce, onions, and brown sugar. Press biscuits into greased muffin cups. Spoon meat mixture into cups. Top with cheese, bake at 400° for 10 minutes.

Phil Ryan, Retired

SAUSAGE JAMBALAYA

- 2 pounds sliced hot sausage
- 1 large minced onion
- 1 minced bell pepper
- 4 ribs chopped celery with leaves
- 2 cloves minced garlic
- 2 cups raw rice
- 1 (16 ounce) can tomatoes
- 3¾ cups water
- 2 cups diced smoked ham
- salt
- red pepper or hot pepper sauce
- thyme
- 3-4 bay leaves
- ¼ cup chopped parsley
- 4 minced green onions with tops

Sauté sausage till cooked. Remove meat. In same oil, sauté onion, bell pepper, celery and garlic. Add rice and tomatoes stirring well. Add liquid and ham. Add spices to taste and add cooked sausage. Bring to boil. Reduce and cook over low heat until rice is cooked, usually 30 to 40 minutes. Stir occasionally to prevent sticking. During last 10 minutes of cooking add parsley and onion. Makes 8 to 10 servings.

Sergeant L. R. "Rocky" Wardlow, Headquarters Company

HELEN'S CHEESE CASSEROLE

- 8-10 canned jalapeños
- 1 pound grated Cheddar cheese
- 6 well-beaten eggs

Cup peppers in half and rinse under cold water. Drain well and chop fine. Spread half of the cheese on bottom of 7x11-inch pan. Sprinkle with chopped peppers. Top with remaining cheese. Pour eggs over all. Bake at 350° for 30 to 40 minutes. Cool 5 to 10 minutes and cut into bite size squares.

Alva Stem, Retired Director of Parks and Recreation Department City of Waco, and wife Helen, Foundation Members

Chow time at the Ranger campsite.

Wild Things

Courtesy of Bill Gunn Collection

Captain Will Wright and Co.

CAPTAIN WILL WRIGHT

Captain Will Wright was born February 19, 1868 in Calwell county. His family moved to Dewitt county when he was a baby and he was raised there. The Rangers were sent to Dewitt county by the governor because of the feud between the Taylor and Sutton families that had gone on since both of the families had moved from Georgia. It had gone on so long it was impossible for any kind of law and order to be maintained. When the Rangers moved in it was Captain McNelly's old company under Captain Red Hill. It was said that McNelly wouldn't enlist a man that wasn't from a good family, so most of his company were from the old south. They were dashing young men who mostly had joined for adventure. These were the men whose influence Will came under as a young boy. The Ranger camp was located close to where Will's father lived, and he spent a lot of time there. He confided to some of them that when he got old enough he'd be a Ranger. Will spent a lot of time as a cowboy and was an excellent rider. This helped him immensely in later years.

Wright moved to Wilson county where he served a short time as Justice of the Peace. He became a Deputy Sheriff under John Craighead. When a vacancy came up in John Rogers Ranger company, the sheriff recommended Wright. He was sent to Cotulla in LaSalle county, which was a tough town. They immediately contested him, but the shot went thru his coat. He drew before his assailant could get off another shot and killed him. This established his reputation among the outlaw element in Cotulla.

In later years he was confronted by a man with a knife who tried to stab him in his heart, but he had a can of Prince Albert Tobacco in his pocket which made his assailant miss his mark.

Wright left the Ranger service and served 15 years as Sheriff of Wilson county. He was an outstanding sheriff and during this time served as president of the Texas Sheriff's Association. After Jim Ferguson was impeached in 1917, Governor Hobby appointed Wright to Ranger Captain and authorized him to form a company to be stationed in Laredo.

In 1918 national prohibition was passed. The 18th Amendment caused a serious problem for Texas. Texas has 1,248 miles of common border with Mexico. This has created problems for many years and a lot of the time it has fallen the duty of the Texas

Rangers to patrol these long stretches along the Rio Grande. Many times they camped for weeks on end, living off the land. Smugglers began bringing in illegal booze from Mexico as soon as prohibition was passed. They were known as "tequileros" and came across every night. It was brought across on pack mules and later transferred to a more modern means of transportation.

Captain Will Wright's company was in one of the strategic locations to patrol the border. The country was extremely rough and practically everything that grew had thorns on it. During prohibition Captain Wright's company destroyed thousands of gallons of illegal spirits and he barely escaped death many times. He was unrelenting in his pursuit of bootleggers.

WILLIAM JESSE "BILL" MCDONALD

William Jesse "Bill" McDonald was born in Mississippi in 1852 and moved to Texas in 1883. McDonald was tried for treason at the age of sixteen because of a conflict with Union authorities, but was acquitted. After graduating in 1872 from Soules Commercial College in New Orleans he taught penmanship in Henderson and started a store on the Sabine River at Brown's Bluff. Later while running a grocery store in Mineola he became a close friend of Justice of the Peace Jim Hogg, who later became Governor of Texas. After becoming a Deputy Sheriff in Wood County he quickly became known as a fearless lawman and a quick shot.

He filed on school land in Hardeman County where he soon became Deputy Sheriff, Special Ranger and Deputy Marshall for the northern district of Texas and the southern district of Kansas.

Governor Hogg made McDonald Captain of Company B Frontier Battalion in January 1891. During this time he had many tough assignments including bank robberies, strikes and race riots. Captain Bill was well known for having lots of nerve in any dangerous situation. He walked into Fort Brown with 25 rebellious black soldiers holding guns on him and said, "Put them guns up." This so surprised the black soldiers that they obeyed his command. One of the Army officers later said, "Bill McDonald would charge Hell with a bucket of water."

A Texas town had asked the Governor to send Rangers to quell a riot. When McDonald

Rangers on back row with captured prisoners on front.
Captain Bill McDonald on far right of back row.

arrived alone the town officials asked him where the others were and McDonald told them that he'd come alone. The officials said, "You mean the Governor only sent one Ranger?" To this McDonald replied, "You don't have but one riot do you?" This is where the saying originated 'ONE RIOT, ONE RANGER'.

Bill was such a well known Ranger and had so much publicity from newspapers and politicians that he was asked to go on a wolf hunt with Theodore Roosevelt. He wasn't too crazy about going with a Republican since he was a staunch Democrat, but it paid off later when Roosevelt wrote a letter which was used in a book written about him. He was later entertained by Roosevelt at the White House.

In 1912 Captain McDonald acted as bodyguard for President Woodrow Wilson who later appointed him Marshall of the northern district of Texas. He died of pneumonia in Wichita Falls, Texas on January 15, 1918 and is buried at Quanah, Texas. Bill's philosophy was that no man in the wrong can stand up against one who is in the right and keeps on coming.

Photo of Texas Rangers on capitol steps —
front row Capt. Bill McDonald fifth from the left.

QUAIL FRIED IN DEEP FAT

12 cleaned quail
1 cup milk
½ cup flour
½ teaspoon salt
⅛ teaspoon black pepper

Pour enough oil into a heavy deep skillet to cover the bottom to a depth of approximately 2 inches. Bring the cooking oil to a high heat. Dip the birds in milk, then roll them in flour mixed with salt and pepper. Place the birds into the skillet, turning to brown evenly. Actual cooking time will be about 3 to 4 minutes.

Roberto D. Garza, Jr., Company D

I was raised in San Isidro which is a small community in Starr County located approximately 35 miles north of Rio Grande City. The people of San Isidro are mostly farmers and ranchers. When I was about thirteen or fourteen years of age, I began to sneak out of the house with my father's old pump-action .22 caliber rifle. The rifle was a Remington model 12-A. Each day when I got home from school, the first thing I would do was take that .22 rifle and walk out back behind several acres of land which was used by an uncle for grazing cattle. I mostly went out to plink or target practice. One late December afternoon, I heard some quail a short distance from the house. I could see two quail sitting on the bottom strand of a barbed wire fence. I quickly sneaked into my father's room to get the rifle. I also took several rounds of .22 caliber shotshells often referred to as "rat shot". I walked along the fence line away from the house. I could still see the birds sitting on the bottom strand of the barbed wire fence. I loaded one round into the chamber of the rifle. The weeds were high and I could not see where the quail were. I carefully crept up to the area where I thought the two birds were. I got within ten to fifteen yards of the area and noticed there was a covey of quail on the ground. I nervously aimed my rifle at the covey and took a "skillet shot" at the birds. Birds flopped in all directions. I scampered about and picked up seven birds from the ground.

Roberto D. Garza, Jr., Company D

GRILLED QUAIL

8 quail
8 jalapeño peppers
8-16 slices bacon

Let us assume that you have just cleaned these birds. Stuff a jalapeño inside each of the birds. Take 1 or 2 strips of bacon and wrap around each quail, using a toothpick to hold the bacon in place. Using mesquite wood, place the birds on the grill making sure they are not directly over the mesquite coals. Allow enough time for the birds to acquire the mesquite smoke flavor. This will take approximately 20 to 30 minutes. Remove from heat and seal tightly in foil. Return to grill and cook until the birds are done to your satisfaction. Birds will be tender with a wonderful flavor.

Roberto D. Garza, Jr.,
Company D

During a Saturday afternoon of one quail season, my friend and I decided to hunt quail. We were still in high school and a bit inexperienced. Quail that season had been rather scarce because of the drought. We were both walking along a brushy area when my friend suddenly jumped a covey of quail and took a shot. One bird fell to the ground and I walked in that direction. I combed the area near some small brush and cactus, but could not find the bird. My friend walked over to help look for the lost bird. After a few minutes of combing the area, I could not believe what I saw. A five-foot Diamondback Rattlesnake had beat us to our kill. The snake had taken the bird into its mouth and was not about to let go. We watched the snake with curiosity and let him have the bird.

Roberto D. Garza, Jr., Company D

BIRDS ROASTED IN THEIR FEATHERS

Open the bird in the usual manner, and draw; then cover with wet clay and bury in hot coals. In 45 minutes draw from the coals and peel off the clay. Feathers and skin will come off at the same time. Delicious when cooked in this manner.

John Barron Harris,
Texas Ranger
Association Foundation,
and wife Cheryl

F.A.'S KILLER DOVE GUMBO

24-36 doves
1 large onion, chopped
2 sticks celery, chopped
1 green bell pepper, chopped
4 cloves garlic, minced
1 tablespoon Worcestershire sauce
1 tablespoon Louisiana Cajun Magic
1 cup margarine
1 cup all-purpose flour
gumbo filé
jalapeño pepper slices
hot pepper sauce
6 green onions, chopped

Boil the doves in 3 quarts of water seasoned with salt and pepper for one hour or until meat falls off the bone. With a sharp paring knife and fork remove the meat from the bone and put it back in the water. Add the onion, celery, bell pepper, garlic, Worcestershire sauce and Cajun Magic. Let this simmer while you make the roux. To make roux melt margarine in a large cast iron skillet. Using medium heat, gradually stir in flour continuously until well mixed. Continue cooking and stirring until the mixture "turns" from a yellow color to a chocolate brown. This takes about 30 minutes. Add the roux to the gumbo mixture and simmer for another hour. Sprinkle filé over the entire surface of pot contents. Add jalapeño pepper slices and pepper sauce to taste. Caution: This stuff goes a long way. Serve gumbo over rice and garnish with chopped green onions.

John Barron Harris,
Texas Ranger
Association Foundation,
and wife Cheryl

RANCHO VERDE CASSEROLE DE LA PALOMA

Roll dove breasts in a blend of garlic powder, salt, pepper and celery salt. Wrap the dove breasts in bacon slices and secure with a toothpick. Wrap the breasts in foil - 4 to a package. Seal and cook in oven at 350° or on grill for 1½ hours. Unwrap, baste with your favorite sauce and smoke for 15 to 20 minutes. Take breasts out of the foil and place in a casserole dish. Remove the toothpicks. Sauté 1 large chopped onion in margarine. Combine with 2 cans of cream of mushroom soup, 1 can chopped green chilies and 1 teaspoon of chili powder. Pour over the dove breasts and cover with thin slices of jalapeño cheese. Place in medium warm oven for 15 minutes or until cheese melts. Garnish with thin slices of sweet pepper, ripe olives and purple onion rings.

John Barron Harris,
Texas Ranger
Association Foundation,
and wife Cheryl

This recipe was given to me by my good friends, Frank and Joyce Green, of Stephenville, Texas.

WILD DUCK

Use a heavy cast iron pot with a tight fitting lid. Wash 3 ducks and sprinkle liberally with salt, pepper, onion salt and garlic salt. Melt ½ stick butter or margarine in pot and brown birds all over. Add 1 cup orange juice. Place the birds on their backs and cover with minced onions. Put lid on pot and simmer very slowly for 45 minutes. Add another cup of orange juice. Turn birds over with breast down, replace lid and cook on low fire for 3 to 3½ hours. Meat should fall off bones.

John Barron Harris,
Texas Ranger
Association Foundation,
and wife Cheryl

12 doves may be substituted for the ducks.

This recipe was given to me in 1989 by Sam Thompson of Clearlake, Texas.

RALPH HARRIS'S WILD TURKEY

- 1 boneless wild turkey breast
- 2 cups Italian dressing
- 1/4 cup hot pepper sauce

Cut breast meat into 1-inch strips. Combine dressing and pepper sauce. Marinate meat 24 hours. Remove from marinade and sprinkle lightly with cayenne pepper, coarse ground black pepper and salt. Place on grill. Cook approximately 8 minutes on each side.

**John Barron Harris,
Texas Ranger
Association Foundation,
and wife Cheryl**

SQUIRREL STEW

One squirrel, dressed and cut into small pieces, three slices of salt pork, three or four ears of green sweet corn, according to size, three or four large tomatoes, two medium onions, two cups shelled fresh butterbeans, three medium size Irish potatoes, two green peppers if you have them. Put the pieces of squirrel and pork into a kettle and cover with cold water. Bring to a boil and simmer slowly. Cut corn from cobs, then chop other vegetables, but not too fine. Season highly with black and red pepper and salt. Let simmer on a slow fire until cooked down thick. The meat should fall from the bones and the vegetables be thoroughly soft. Be careful not to scorch.

**John Barron Harris,
Texas Ranger
Association Foundation,
and wife Cheryl**

PAT'S CAMP MULLIGAN

Take beef, deer, squirrel or any other kind of meat that is desired or available; potatoes, tomatoes, onions or any other vegetable that is desired or available; and any kind of seasoning that is desired and available. Cut it all up and put it in a big pot (you can use a foot tub if you don't have a pot). Place on a camp fire or stove and cook until done.

**Sergeant Joe W. Haralson,
Company A**

This recipe is from my Uncle Pat Haralson.

VENISON EMPANADAS

1 pound ground venison
½ cup margarine
2 large chopped onions
½ cup chopped olives
½ cup chopped celery
2 chopped jalapeño peppers
salt & pepper
2 tablespoons vinegar
1 small can tomato sauce
2 tablespoons Worcestershire sauce

Brown meat in margarine. Add remaining ingredients and simmer. Cool, make favorite pie pastry, cut in circles (about the size of a cup). Place meat mixture in center and fold over, prick with a fork. Place on greased cookie sheet and bake in moderate oven for 20 to 30 minutes.

Captain Walter A. "Bob" Werner, Retired, and wife Jeanne

LOST PINES VENISON CHILI

6 slices bacon
2 pounds ground venison
1 large chopped onion
3 cups water
28 ounces undrained canned tomatoes
1 tablespoon chili powder
1 teaspoon pepper
1 teaspoon salt
1 teaspoon cumin
1 teaspoon garlic powder
16 ounces undrained canned kidney beans

Cut bacon into ½-inch pieces. Cook in a Dutch oven until crisp. Remove bacon and set aside. Add venison and onion to Dutch oven with bacon drippings. Cook over medium heat until brown. Drain off drippings. Add bacon and next 7 ingredients. Bring to boil. Cover, reduce heat and simmer for 1 hour, stirring occasionally. Add beans, cover and cook an additional 30 minutes.

Sergeant L. R. "Rocky" Wardlow, Headquarters Company

JERKED VENISON OR BEEF

The early settlers, had no means of refrigerating a whole beef or venison during the summer season, a whole animal being too much for a family to use while the meat was still fresh, they ingenuously borrowed the process of jerking or drying the meat from the Indians. In this manner the four quarters and ribs of an animal could be kept perfectly for twelve months, if necessary. The animal was killed, dressed and quartered. The bones from the fore and hind quarters were removed by making a straight slit down the sides with a sharp knife. Then began the process of stripping, or cutting the meat into ribbon-like pieces, except the ribs, which were hung out to dry without removing the bones. The boneless fore and hind quarters were cut in long strips 1-inch or 1½-inch thick, leaving the strips fastened together at alternate ends, thus having one continuous length instead of numerous short ones. The meat was then salted and peppered. After the sun was well up in the morning the long strips and the ribs were hung on a line in the sun to dry. It was brought indoors each night to prevent the dew from falling on it, it being of the utmost importance that the meat be kept absolutely dry. The rush would be great to get the meat under cover if a rain cloud appeared. The meat would be perfectly cured, or dried, within 3 or 4 days - the length depending upon the time of year and the heat from the sun. When cured, it was stored away in clean cloth bags to be used as needed. In preparing jerked or dried meat for cooking, it is first soaked for several hours, cut in pieces as for steak, and smothered in gravy and onions as Swiss steak. The cowboys and rangers found jerked beef a convenient food to carry on trips taking them from home several days at a time.

John Barron Harris,
Texas Ranger
Association Foundation,
and wife Cheryl

VENISON FOIL DINNER

Slice venison into ¼-inch slices. Prepare, wash and slice vegetables - potatoes, onions, carrots and green peppers (any favorite veggies may be substituted). Seal venison and vegetables in foil. Sprinkle with salt, pepper and garlic salt. This can be grilled or placed in the oven.

Sid Merchant, Retired

BANKERS DELIGHT

7 pounds lean stew meat
4 pounds lean venison
2 pounds chicken livers
salt
3 teaspoon red pepper
3 teaspoon black pepper
1 bottle hot pepper sauce
1 large bottle Worcestershire sauce
1 box barley
4 pounds chopped potatoes
2 large chopped green peppers
3 cans cream style corn
3 bunches green onions
2 pods chopped garlic
1 pound brown sugar
1½ pounds uncooked rice
spaghetti

Put stew meat, venison and chicken livers into water, covering about 1 to 2 inches and add salt, pepper, pepper sauce, Worcestershire and barley. Cook at slow boil about 2 hours. Remove meat and cut very fine. Replace in water and continue cooking, adding water as needed to keep ingredients well covered. Add potatoes, green peppers and corn. Cook slowly. Cut up tops and all of green onions. Add onions and garlic. Check water to cover. Cook about 1 hour. Taste for flavor as to salt and pepper. If it is too hot, don't worry about it as further additions will cool it down. If not hot enough, add a little more pepper and pepper sauce. Next add brown sugar and continue cooking for 30 to 40 minutes at a slow boil. Check for flavor again and add rice. Keep well covered with water and soon the ingredients will start going into solution. Check for flavor. The last thing to add is spaghetti in about 2-inch lengths. This is what you use to take up any too much fluid. I do believe the secret to this is good materials, slow cooking, addition of sugar. Along the way, while this is cooking, you can add Worcestershire until 1½ to 2 bottles have been used. This must be stirred to keep from sticking to bottom.

Lewis C. Rigler, Retired

MEDALLIONS OF VENISON

Cut back strap of venison in ¾-inch medallions. Wrap with bacon like a filet. Secure bacon with a toothpick. Marinate in Italian Salad Dressing for several hours. Grill approximately 6 to 8 minutes per side. Be sure not to overcook. Serve with a heated mixture of equal parts Red Currant jelly and Dijon mustard.

Charles Schreiner III and wife Karol

VENISON MINCEMEAT

- 1 orange
- 1 lemon
- 2 pounds lean venison, cooked and coarsely chopped
- ½ pound beef suet, cooked and coarsely chopped
- 5 pounds apples, chopped, not peeled
- 3 pounds raisins
- 1 tablespoon salt
- 2 cups brown sugar
- 5 cups apple cider
- 1 cup beef broth
- 2½ pints grape juice
- ½ teaspoon black pepper
- 2 teaspoons ground cloves
- 2 teaspoons cinnamon
- ¾ cup white vinegar
- 1 teaspoon mace
- 2 teaspoons allspice
- 2 teaspoons nutmeg
- 1 cup molasses

Seed orange and lemon, then grind peel, juice and all. Mix meat, suet, apples, raisins, salt, sugar, cider and beef broth. Let come to a boil. Reduce heat and simmer for 1 hour. Add remaining ingredients. Bring to a boil for 10 minutes, stirring often. Pack in sterile jars and process. Be sure and don't use any fat from the deer meat.

John Barron Harris, Texas Ranger Association Foundation, and wife Cheryl

VENISON STROGANOFF

- 1 pound venison steak cut in long, thin strips
- 3 tablespoons flour dash of salt and pepper
- 1 onion, chopped
- 1 cup tomato juice
- 1½ cups water
- 1 teaspoon sugar
- 1 can mushrooms
- ½ cup sour cream

Dredge meat with flour, salt and pepper. Brown lightly in fat with the onion. Add tomato juice, water and sugar. Simmer until tender. Ten minutes before serving, add mushrooms and sour cream. Yield: 4 servings.

John Barron Harris,
Texas Ranger
Association Foundation,
and wife Cheryl

WINE ROASTED VENISON

- 6-9 pound venison roast
- bacon slices
- 1 teaspoon salt
- ¼ teaspoon pepper
- 2 tablespoons chopped onion
- garlic (optional)
- ¼ cup lemon juice
- 1 cup beef bouillon
- 1 cup Burgundy

Place roast on rack in shallow roasting pan. Arrange bacon slices over roast and sear in oven for ten minutes at 500°. Remove from oven and lower oven temperature to 400°. Combine remaining ingredients, pour over roast and cover with foil. Cook, basting occasionally with pan drippings until meat is tender.

John Barron Harris,
Texas Ranger
Association Foundation,
and wife Cheryl

RATTLESNAKE

Skin, clean and cut into bite-size pieces. Season and dip in sour milk. Combine cornmeal and a small amount of flour. Stir in salt, pepper and a little cayenne pepper. Dip meat pieces in beer, then roll in cornmeal mixture. Fry like fish in hot grease.

John Barron Harris,
Texas Ranger
Association Foundation,
and wife Cheryl

ARMADILLO STEW

- 1 armadillo; shelled, cleaned and cut into chunks
- 1 pound dried pinto beans, cleaned and soaked
- 1 large onion, chopped garlic, chili powder, cumin, cilantro, salt and pepper to taste

Sauté meat in oil. Add beans, onion and seasonings to meat. Cover with water. Cook until beans are done. May need to add more water. Yield: 8 servings.

John Barron Harris, Texas Ranger Association Foundation, and wife Cheryl

POSSUM AND SWEET POTATOES

Dress a fat young possum and cut in half by splitting down back and underside. Place in roaster with ¾ cup water, after salting the meat. Peel and cut in halves 3 medium yam potatoes. Place around the possum and bake until the meat is tender and brown. If the possum is fat, no butter or lard is necessary to season. Serve hot with the potatoes and gravy in the pan.

John Barron Harris, Texas Ranger Association Foundation, and wife Cheryl

MOUNTAIN OYSTERS

Wash calf fries and peel off outer membrane. Slice lengthwise and peel off inner membrane. Sprinkle with salt. Roll in ½ cornmeal, ½ flour mixture. Pan fry in iron skillet at 350° with 1 inch of oil. Brown on both sides only turning once. Drain and serve hot with dipping sauce. For sauce mix 1 teaspoon horseradish, ½ cup ketchup and ½ cup barbecue sauce.

John Barron Harris, Texas Ranger Association Foundation, and wife Cheryl

RABBIT ENCHILADAS

- 1 tablespoon corn oil
- 1 large onion, chopped
- chopped garlic to taste (optional)
- ½ teaspoon salt
- 1 tablespoon chili powder
- ½ teaspoon ground cumin
- 3 medium tomatoes, peeled and diced
- 2 cups chopped, cooked rabbit
- ½ cup rabbit stock
- 1½ cups grated sharp Cheddar, Monterey Jack or cheese of your choice
- 8 warm corn or flour tortillas
- cilantro, shredded lettuce, salsa (optional)

Heat oil in skillet. Add onion and garlic. Cook till tender. Add salt, chili powder and cumin. Mix well. Add tomatoes, meat and stock. Mix well and simmer for 5 minutes. Add ¾ cup of the cheese and mix thoroughly. Fill a tortilla with the mixture, roll up and place seam side down in a greased 7x12-inch baking pan. Spoon any remaining sauce evenly over enchiladas and sprinkle remaining cheese over top. Cover and bake at 350° for 25 minutes. Serve with chopped cilantro, shredded lettuce and salsa, if desired. Yield: Serves 4 to 8.

John Barron Harris,
Texas Ranger
Association Foundation,
and wife Cheryl

FISH BAKED IN CLAY

Rub a fish in soft clay. Let it stand awhile, then roll it in clay until it is completely covered. Let clay dry; then bury fish in hot coals and ashes for an hour. Rake out, crack the clay; remove skin and dust with salt.

John Barron Harris,
Texas Ranger
Association Foundation,
and wife Cheryl

HERB-GRILLED TROUT

- 6 trout or other firm-fleshed fish steaks (1 to 1½ pounds each)
- 1 cup lemon juice
- ⅔ cup oil
- 3 tablespoons onion powder
- 2½ teaspoons salt
- 2 teaspoons garlic powder
- 1 teaspoon ground black pepper
- 3 tablespoons parsley flakes

If using trout, make slits on top of both sides of each fish. Place fish closely together in a small baking dish. Combine lemon juice, oil, onion powder, salt, garlic powder and black pepper. Mix well. Stir in parsley flakes and pour over fish. Cover and refrigerate 1 hour or longer, turning once. Cook fish on greased grill over hot charcoal. Reserve marinade. Grill about 10 minutes or until fish flakes when tested with a fork, turning once and brushing frequently with marinade.

John Barron Harris,
Texas Ranger
Association Foundation,
and wife Cheryl

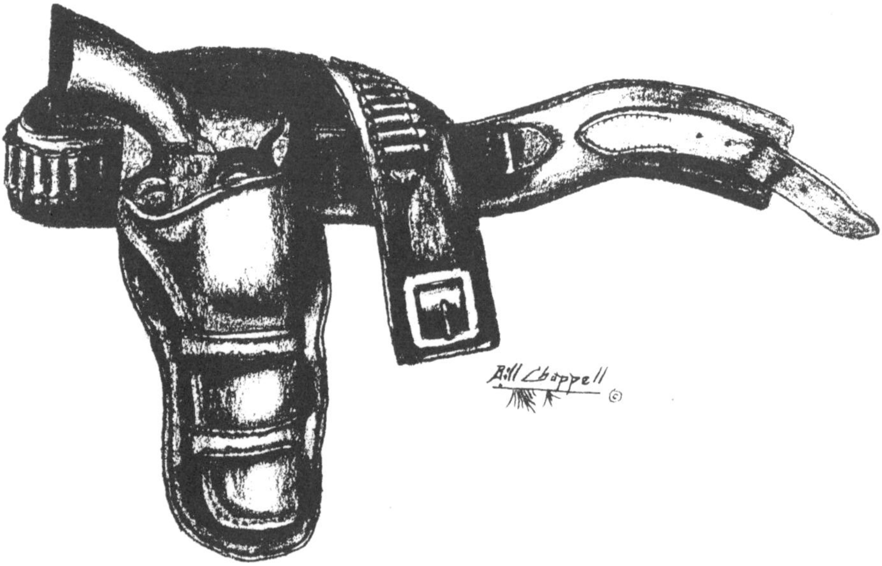

Colt Frontier model "Six Shooter" with double loop holster abnd money belt.

When I was a very young boy I had a garden on some land that had been my grandfather Barron's cow lot. I raised a lot of good vegetables and sold them out of a little red wagon to the neighbors. One of my best customers was Mrs. John Sealy (Celeste) Caldwell who lived across the street. The Caldwells had been in the jewelry business for many years in Bryan. During the height of the Bonnie and Clyde era a member of their gang, Whitey Walker, robbed and kidnapped the Caldwells. They were taken to the Navasota River Bottom and tied to a tree with barbed wire. As soon as I heard this I rushed over to see Mrs. Caldwell and to look at the scratches on her wrists where she had been tied.

Walker was later captured and brought back to Bryan to stand trial. Bonnie and Clyde had broken so many of their gang members out of jail and the penitentiary that this gave Brazos County officials much concern. They placed search lights all around the jail and posted guards outside. This was quite a show and all the towns people would drive by at night to look up where the cells were to try and see the outlaw. When they finally tried Walker the courtroom was full of spectators. My granddaddy Harris was on the jury.

John Barron Harris, Texas Ranger Association Foundation

★ ★ ★ ★

Rabbit Food & Kettle Brew

CAPTAIN M. T. "LONE WOLF" GONZAULLAS

Lone Wolf was born in Cadiz, Spain on July 4, 1891. His mother was German and his father either Spanish or Portuguese. In the book "Lone Wolf" by Brownson Malsch he says Gonzaullas is of Spanish descent. Other books say his father was Portuguese. Very little is known about his childhood or early life. His parents had variously been reported killed in the Galveston Hurricane of 1900 or wounded by bandits when his brothers were killed in their border home in El Paso. No one seems to know anything about him until he joined the Rangers at age 29 on October 1, 1920.

He was reported to be in the Mexican Army and a mercenary in the Chinese Army, but no one seems to really know. It's not known how many men he killed in the line of duty since he would never tell. He also would never tell how many gunshots and other wounds that he himself had suffered. He was a very religious man, a staunch Presbyterian and very active in his church. It was his practice to give away New Testament Bibles to those he thought would read them. He inscribed passages for them to read in red ink.

Gonzaullas was always one of the best dressed Rangers in history. He liked hand tooled holsters and gun belts, guns decorated with silver and gold, and some set with diamonds. He was a Mason and a member of the Blue Lodge, Shriners and Scottish Rite. Some of his guns had these emblems on them as well as being engraved with various sayings. The pistols he carried had the trigger guard cut away so as to make them faster to draw and shoot.

After joining the Rangers he was sent to Wichita County to help bring some kind of order to the booming oilfield towns of north Texas. Murder, robbery, gambling, bootlegging and prostitution were so rampant that local officials were unable to stop them. Lone Wolf was so active in bringing law and order to the oilfield that it wasn't long before the very mention of his name

would bring shudders to the outlaw element. He broke up hundreds of stills and poured out thousands of gallons of illegal booze.

When Mirian "Maw" Ferguson took office in January 1933, she fired all the Rangers that hadn't already quit. Lone Wolf and another Ranger acted as her guard for the inauguration as Governor. The next day they were all fired. Lone Wolf went to work as a security man for Atlas Pipeline Company and Spartan Refining Company in east Texas. He was instrumental in hiring 18 other former Rangers for the company. He went to work for the District Attorney in Longview as Special Investigator and immediately got results in getting indictments on gamblers and bootleggers.

In 1935 when James V. Alred took office as governor he got the Legislature to pass laws establishing the Department of Public Safety. At this time the Rangers and the Highway Patrol were merged into one law enforcement body. M. T. Gonzaullas was named head of the Department of Intelligence. As department head he became responsible for detective, plain clothes and undercover investigations. He visited all the modern laboratories in Washington and in other cities where they had been established. He set up the first department in Texas to analyze information on fingerprints, handwriting, ballistics and a laboratory to completely check out all types of evidence. At this point in history the Rangers entered into modern methods of criminology and began a new era of law enforcement in Texas.

Lone Wolf decided to retire at age 60 after almost 30 years as a Ranger and to assume a new career as a consultant for radio, movies and television. He became technical advisor to Stacy Keach who was to produce "Tales of the Texas Rangers". In the long and illustrious history of the Texas Rangers Lone Wolf certainly occupies one of the most colorful places. On February 13, 1977, Lone Wolf passed away with his wife Laura holding his hand; he took with him the knowledge of how many times he'd been wounded and how many men he'd killed in the line of duty.

CAPTAIN FRANK HAMER

Captain Frank Hamer was born on March 17, 1884, in Wilson County, Texas. In 1890 his family moved to San Saba County where Frank attended public school, such as there were in those days. This was when San Saba County was still very sparsely inhabited. Wildlife was plentiful. Frank spent much of his time hunting and fishing. Sometimes he would spend weeks out with only a rifle, fishing pole, knife and blanket. He learned all the animal and bird sounds and became an excellent caller. He was also a crack shot with a rifle and pistol, and could throw a knife with such force that it would kill an armadillo and pin it to the ground. From living in the wild he developed a keen sense of hearing, tracking, smell and sight to the point that he was almost as good as an Indian. This keen sense of perception aided him greatly when he was on the trail of Bonnie and Clyde.

Movie star Tom Mix with Capt. Frank Hammer standing on his right.

Hamer was working in west Texas as a ranch hand on a ranch between Sheffield and Fort Stockton when he got word that two horses, saddles and bridles had been stolen on a neighboring ranch. He was listening on a party line telephone and heard the Sheriff trying to get someone to try and intercept the horse thief. The man the Sheriff had called declined and Hamer broke in on the conversation and asked if he could try and catch the horse thief. Frank knew the country well enough to know that the man would have to stop and water his horse. He hid by a windmill and when the thief showed up he captured him and started back to town with him. He met the Sheriff on the way back to town and the Sheriff was very impressed with the young cowboy. The Sheriff recommended Frank to the Rangers and in April of 1906 Captain J. H. Rogers wrote that he'd been accepted and to report to Sergeant Jim Moore at Sheffield, Texas. He was 22 years old.

From this time on Frank was in and out of the Texas Ranger Service. He left the service several times to go to better paying law enforcement jobs, but always returned to the Rangers. When Lee Simmons, Texas Prison System manager, was asked to find someone to track down Bonnie and Clyde he immediately chose Hamer. At this time Frank had quit the Ranger Service, as had most of the regulars because of the political corruption in the Governor's office. Governor Maw Ferguson accepted Simmons recommendation and Hamer was given the job. This became one of the most famous manhunts in law enforcement history. It is still famous today because of the movie 'Bonnie and Clyde' that was made in the 1970's.

Hamer was commissioned as a highway patrolman and the pursuit of Bonnie and Clyde lasted 102 days. Hamer followed their trail from February 10 until they were finally killed on May 23, 1934. Captain Hamer used every instinct he had ever learned in tracking Bonnie and Clyde. He learned all the back roads they traveled, what kind of whiskey they drank, what they smoked and where they slept at night. On April 14 highway patrol Chief Phares told Hamer he was going to give him a man to travel with him. Hamer requested he hire B. M. Gault who had served with him in the Rangers. Hamer learned through an informant that Clyde picked up his mail on a country road near Plain Dealing, Louisiana. Hamer informed Sheriff Henderson Jordan of his plan. Bob Alcorn and Ted Hinton from the Dallas Sheriff's office were also members of Hamer's party that were to meet Barrow as he picked up his mail. Along with Deputy Oakley from Bienville Parish, Louisiana. Hamer chose Sheriff Jordan, his deputy and their parish location because they were known to be honest and dependable men, in contrast to some other parishes in Louisiana at that time.

The place that Clyde picked up his mail was a stump on the west side of a country road which gave him a view from every direction. Hamer and his men put up a blind on the high side of the road so that they could lay in wait. Hamer placed the men at ten foot intervals. If Bonnie and Clyde got by all the men, Hinton was placed on the end with a Browning machine gun so he could step out and blow up the motor on the car. It was agreed that if at all possible they would try and take Bonnie and Clyde alive. The stakeout was made before daylight and there was very little traffic on the road. A little after 9:00 they heard a car coming down the road at high speed. The car came into view at about a thousand yards, still coming fast, but started to slow down as it approached the stump. They immediately recognized Bonnie and Clyde and knew there was no mistake.

At the command "Stick 'em up" Bonnie and Clyde both grabbed guns or had guns in their hands already. All six men began to fire at once. Clyde let out the clutch and the car rolled down into a ditch. Hamer looked at his watch and it was 9:20 AM. This ended a career in which Bonnie and Clyde had killed fifteen men. I can remember very well how relieved everyone was when we heard on the radio that Bonnie and Clyde were no longer a menace.

Hamer was a man who never sought any personal publicity and in fact did everything he could to avoid it. He did not allow the people of Austin to give him a dinner or do anything to commend his efforts. He was a man of absolute honesty and never deviated from this. Hamer died a peaceful death in 1955. He was said to carry to the grave with him many scars, twenty three gunshot wounds and sixteen bullets in his body.

This was Bonnie Parker's shotgun that she killed a highway patrolman with at Grapevine, Texas.

Party of Rangers that finally subdued Bonnie and Clyde.

My mother, Artie Harris, and my aunt, Mrs. W. E. Neeley, took my cousin, Bonnie Mary Neeley, and me to Huntsville to hear Eleanor Roosevelt speak. When we got out of the program we heard that Bonnie and Clyde had helped some of their gang escape from one of the prison farms near Huntsville. Bonnie and Clyde were so in the news in those days that this scared my cousin, Bonnie Mary, and me so bad that we rode all the way back to Bryan riding on the floorboard in the back seat of the car. We just knew they would get us. We never realized that the car we were in wasn't anything they would be interested in, and they sure wouldn't want two little kids.

John Barron Harris,
Texas Ranger Association Foundation

CORNBREAD SALAD

- 4 cups cornbread
- ½ cup chopped onion
- ½ cup chopped celery
- ¼ cup sliced olives
- ½ cup chopped bell pepper
- ¾ cup chopped tomato
- 1 pint mayonnaise

Mix first 6 ingredients together. Add mayonnaise (more or less depending on your taste and the amount of cornbread). Salt and pepper to taste. Mexican cornbread can be used. Also, you can improvise — I have added bacon bits, cubed cheese and pimientos.

Jack Van Cleve, Retired, and wife La Vane

BOB'S CORNBREAD SALAD

- 2 packages cornbread mix
- 1 pound bacon
- 1 cup chopped onion
- 1 cup chopped bell pepper
- 1 cup chopped celery
- 1 large tomato, chopped
- 1½ cups salad dressing
- 4 boiled, chopped eggs

Prepare cornbread according to package directions. Crumble cornbread into a large bowl. Fry bacon till crisp. Add chopped vegetables, salad dressing and eggs. Crumble bacon and stir into above mixture.

Capt. Bob Prince, Retired

COBB SALAD

- 6 cups shredded lettuce
- 6 slices bacon
- 3 cups cooked, chopped chicken
- 3 hard-cooked eggs, chopped
- 2 medium tomatoes, seeded, and chopped
- ¾ cup crumbled blue cheese
- 1 medium avocado
- 1 small stalk Belgian endive
- 1 recipe Brown Derby Dressing

Place lettuce on six individual plates. Fry bacon slices crisp, drain and crumble. Evenly divide chicken, eggs, tomatoes, cheese and bacon among plates, arranging each in a row on top of lettuce. Peel, halve and seed avocado. Cut into wedges. Place avocado wedges and endive leaves to the side. Serve with Brown Derby Dressing. Serves 6.

Captain Jack Dean, Company D, and wife Janie

BROWN DERBY DRESSING

- 1/3 cup red wine vinegar
- 1 tablespoon lemon juice
- 1 teaspoon Worcestershire sauce
- 1/2 teaspoon salt
- 1/2 teaspoon sugar
- 1/2 teaspoon dry mustard
- 1/2 teaspoon black pepper
- 1 clove minced garlic
- 1/2 cup olive oil

Combine all ingredients except olive oil in screw-top jar. Shake to mix well. Add oil, cover and shake vigorously. Chill thoroughly. Shake before serving. Yield: 1 cup of dressing.

**Captain Jack Dean,
Company D,
and wife Janie**

SPINACH SALAD

- 1 bunch fresh spinach
- 1 sliced red onion
- 1 small carton cottage cheese
- 1 cup mayonnaise
- 1/2 cup Italian dressing
- 1/4 cup Parmesan cheese
- bacon bits

Wash spinach, drain well. Tear into bite-size pieces. Separate onion into rings. Add to spinach. Add cottage cheese and toss until thoroughly mixed. Mix together mayonnaise, Italian dressing, cheese and bacon bits. Add to salad just before serving.

Anonymous Texas Ranger

LETTUCE TOSS

- 4 slices diced bacon
- 4 cups leaf lettuce
- 1 large diced tomato
- 1/4 cup sliced green onion
- 1/2 teaspoon salt
- 1/4 teaspoon black pepper
- 2 tablespoons vinegar

Fry bacon until crisp. Drain, reserving 1 tablespoon drippings. Meanwhile, tear lettuce into bowl; add tomato and onion. Sprinkle greens with seasonings. Combine vinegar and bacon drippings, bring to boil. Pour over salad, tossing lightly to mix. Crumble bacon over top of salad. Serve immediately. Yield: 6 servings.

**Captain Jack Dean,
Company D,
and wife Janie**

MARINATED VEGETABLE SALAD

- ¾ cup vinegar
- ½ cup oil
- 1 teaspoon salt
- 1¼ cups sugar
- 1 tablespoon water
- 1 teaspoon black pepper
- 1 (16 ounce) can French-style green beans, drained
- 1 (17 ounce) can English peas, drained
- 1 (12 ounce) can whole corn, drained
- 1 small jar pimientos, drained
- 1 cup chopped celery
- 1 green pepper, chopped
- 1 bunch green onions, chopped

Combine vinegar, oil, salt, sugar, water and pepper in saucepan. Bring to a boil, stirring to dissolve sugar. Cool. Combine the vegetables and stir into cooled vinegar mixture. Cover and place in the refrigerator for 12 hours, stirring occasionally. This will keep forever in the refrigerator.

Cheryl Harris,
Texas Ranger
Association Foundation

My dad, Barney Ward Jr., gave me this wonderful recipe. He likes to add a few hot peppers to his recipe.

LAYERED SALAD

- 1 head lettuce
- 1-2 sliced onions
- 1 pound cooked, crumbled bacon
- 6 sliced, hard-boiled eggs
- 1 package uncooked, frozen peas
- 1 cup mayonnaise
- 1 cup Miracle Whip
- grated cheese

Wash and dry lettuce. Tear into pieces and cover bottom of bowl. Separate onion into rings. Layer in order: bacon, eggs, peas and onions. Mix in a small bowl the mayonnaise and Miracle Whip. Pour mixture over the above layered ingredients. Sprinkle with lots of grated cheese. Refrigerate 24 hours or fix very early in the morning before serving for supper. You can add bell pepper and celery to salad and this makes it very good.

Sergeant Donald R. Morris,
Company A,
and wife Phyllis

SLAW SALAD

12 cups shredded cabbage
1 large chopped green pepper
1 large chopped onion
1 teaspoon celery seed
1½ cups sugar
⅞ cup vinegar
⅞ cup oil
1 teaspoon salt

Combine cabbage, green pepper and onion in a large bowl. In a saucepan, combine sugar, vinegar, oil and salt. Bring to a boil. Drizzle over vegetable mixture. Refrigerate till ready to serve.

Cathy Brumbalow
Office Manager
Harris Farms

CABBAGE WITH GOLDEN NUGGETS

8 ounces shredded coconut
8 ounces small cubes pineapple
16 ounces red cabbage shredded fine
½ cup heavy cream
8 ounces mayonnaise

Combine first three ingredients, toss well and chill. Before serving, whip cream until stiff and fold in mayonnaise and mix.

Edith Kidd
Texas Ranger
Association Foundation
Member

Sounds horrible, but it is really a great and pretty salad.

SHOEPEG CORN SALAD

1 can shoepeg corn
1 can sweet peas
1 can French style green beans
1 cup chopped celery
6 chopped green onions with tops
1 small jar pimientos
1 large chopped green pepper
½ cup oil
1 cup sugar
¾ cup vinegar
1 tablespoon water
1 teaspoon salt
1 teaspoon black pepper

Combine vegetables in a bowl. Mix together oil, sugar, vinegar, water and spices. Bring to a boil. Pour over vegetables. Chill till ready to serve.

Cathy Brumbalow
Office Manager
Harris Farms

ENGLISH PEA SALAD

2 cups lettuce, shredded fine
4-6 hard-boiled eggs, chopped
½ cup chopped sweet pickles
1 small onion, chopped fine
1 small can English peas, drained
dash garlic powder
salt
black pepper
2 heaping tablespoons Miracle Whip

Combine all ingredients. Season to taste. Toss well.

Cheryl Harris,
Texas Ranger
Association Foundation

This recipe has been enjoyed by many on picnic adventures into the mountains when I was a child. My Mother Pauline always took along a small dish-tub and a cover cloth to place in the cold mountain streams to keep food cool until we were ready for lunch.

RANCH HAND POTATO SALAD

4 pounds potatoes
1 (22 ounce) jar sweet pickle relish, undrained
1 (4 ounce) jar chopped pimientos, drained
1 large chopped onion
3 tablespoons celery seed
1 tablespoon black pepper
2 teaspoons salt
1 teaspoon paprika
2 teaspoons prepared mustard
1 (16 ounce) jar Miracle Whip
4 hard-boiled eggs, chopped (optional)

Wash whole potatoes. Boil in jackets until done. Drain and cool. When cool, remove skins and cube in 1-inch squares in a very large bowl. Add relish, pimientos, onion, celery seed, pepper, salt, paprika, mustard, Miracle Whip and eggs. Stir until well mixed. Chill several hours.

Cheryl Harris,
Texas Ranger
Association Foundation

This was an old standby recipe one of my German-Czech friends, Patsy Rickert, used at family gatherings. She took pity on a 20 year old who burned everything and taught me how to cook several German-style dishes that my family still enjoys.

CHICKEN - TUNA SALAD

1 can white tuna
2 cooked chicken breasts
boiled eggs
sweet relish
lots of mayonnaise
1 can small English peas

Mix first five ingredients together. Just before serving, add English peas.

Alva Stem, Retired Director of Parks and Recreation Department City of Waco, and wife Helen, Foundation Members

SHRIMP SALAD

1 medium head cauliflower
thawed, chopped salad shrimp
¼ cup chopped sweet pickles
¼ cup chopped celery
¼ cup chopped stuffed ripe olives
4 boiled, chopped eggs
chopped pimientos
salt & pepper
1 part thick French dressing
1 part Miracle Whip
dash hot pepper sauce
lemon juice
minced garlic

Pull cauliflower apart into flowerets. Place shrimp, pickles, celery, cauliflower, olives, eggs and pimientos into a large bowl. Salt and pepper to taste. For dressing, mix together the French dressing and the Miracle Whip. Add pepper sauce, lemon juice and garlic to taste. Mix well and pour over shrimp mixture. Stir all together. Serve on lettuce leaves with crackers. Yield: 4 servings

Bill Gunn, Retired, and wife Sugar

PISTACHIO SALAD

1 medium tub frozen whipped topping
1 package instant pistachio pudding mix
1 large can crushed pineapple
1½ cups miniature marshmallows

Mix all ingredients together in a bowl and chill. Great with Thanksgiving Dinner and ham.

Sergeant Danny Rhea, Company B, and wife Sue

FRUIT SALAD

- 8 ounces cream cheese
- 1 large can fruit cocktail
- 1 can pineapple chunks
- 3 tablespoons pineapple juice
- 30 marshmallows

Soften and mash cream cheese. Drain fruit cocktail and pineapple chunks reserving 3 tablespoons pineapple juice. Melt marshmallows in pineapple juice (microwave or over low heat). Remove and add cream cheese. Combine with fruit. Pour into a 9x9-inch square dish and set overnight in refrigerator. Serve on crisp lettuce leaf.

Sergeant Morgan L. Miller, Company D, and wife Ann

Add a can of drained mandarin oranges for a little tartness and 1 cup chopped pecans if desired.

APRICOT SALAD

- ¼ cup sugar
- 1 (3 ounce) package orange Jello
- 1 cup apricot nectar
- 8 ounces cream cheese, softened
- 1 can crushed pineapple
- 1 cup grated carrots
- 1 cup chopped pecans
- 4 ounces frozen whipped topping

Dissolve sugar and Jello in hot nectar. Cool until congealed. Fold in cream cheese, pineapple, carrots, pecans and whipped topping. Chill until set.

Capt. Bob Prince, Retired

ORANGE JELLO SALAD

- 1 (3 ounce) package orange Jello
- 8 ounces small curd cottage cheese
- 8 ounces frozen whipped topping
- 8 ounces crushed, drained pineapple
- 8 ounces drained mandarin oranges

Prepare Jello according to package directions. When slightly set, add cottage cheese. Fold in whipped topping, then pineapple and mandarin oranges. Chill and serve.

Lloyd Johnson, Retired

PINEAPPLE SALAD

- 1 envelope Knox gelatin
- ¼ cup cold water
- 1 large can pineapple, crushed
- ½ cup sugar
- 1 lemon, juiced
- 1 cup grated Cheddar cheese
- 1 pint cream, whipped

Dissolve gelatin in cold water. Stir over hot water to finish dissolving. Boil pineapple, sugar and lemon juice together for a minute. Stir gelatin into it. Let cool until it begins to thicken, then add grated cheese. Last, fold in cream.

John Barron Harris, Texas Ranger Association Foundation, and wife Cheryl

This recipe came from Mrs. Herman Dobbs mother of one of my best friends, Tom Dobbs.

PINK SALAD

- 1 large tub frozen whipped topping
- 1 can cherry pie filling
- 1 can sweetened condensed milk
- 1 small can drained, crushed pineapple
- 1 can drained mandarin oranges
- 2 cups miniature marshmallows
- ¼ cup coconut
- ¼ cup chopped pecans

Mix whipped topping, pie filling and sweetened condensed milk until well blended. Add pineapple, oranges, marshmallows, coconut and pecans. Blend well. Make the night before serving and refrigerate for best results. Serves 16.

Captain Bob Mitchell, Retired, and wife Jerry

My experience with chain letters has not been very successful, but many years ago I participated in a recipe chain letter. Mrs. Ladelle Cole of McAllen, mother-in-law of retired Ranger Frank Horger, sent me this recipe, which became an immediate hit with my family.

CRANBERRY SALAD

- 1 large box raspberry Jello
- 1 cup boiling water
- 1 small can crushed pineapple, drained
- 1 can whole berry cranberry sauce
- ¾ cup grape juice
- 8 ounces cream cheese
- ½ cup sugar
- ½ cup Miracle Whip
- ¾ cup nuts, chopped

Dissolve Jello in boiling water. Add pineapple, cranberry sauce and grape juice. Pour into a 9x13-inch dish and chill. Whip cream cheese, sugar and Miracle Whip together. Spread over chilled salad and top with nuts.

John Barron Harris, Texas Ranger Association Foundation, and wife Cheryl

CHRISTMAS SALAD

- 1 large package strawberry Jello
- 1 cup boiling water
- 1 tray ice cubes
- 1 can whole cranberry sauce
- 1 can crushed pineapple, drained
- 1 cup chopped pecans
- 1 cup miniature marshmallows
- ½ pint whipping cream

Dissolve Jello in water. Add ice cubes. When it starts to gel remove remaining ice. Stir in cranberry sauce, pineapple, pecans and marshmallows. Chill well before serving, whip whipping cream, and fold into Jello mixture.

John Barron Harris, Texas Ranger Association Foundation, and wife Cheryl

7 CUP SALAD

- 1 cup sliced seedless grapes or fruit cocktail
- 1 cup mandarin oranges or 1 large orange chopped
- 1 cup coconut
- 1 cup sour cream or whipped whipping cream
- 1 cup crushed pineapple
- 1 cup miniature marshmallows
- 2 sliced bananas
- 1 cup pecans

Combine all ingredients. Serve on lettuce leaves, on a cake or in sherbert dishes. Top with a cherry.

John Barron Harris, Texas Ranger Association Foundation, and wife Cheryl

STRAWBERRY GELATIN SALAD

- 2 (3 ounce) packages strawberry-banana flavored gelatin
- 2 cups boiling water
- 2 (10 ounce) packages frozen sliced strawberries
- 1 (13½ ounce) can crushed pineapple
- 2 large ripe bananas, peeled and finely diced
- ½ cup pecan halves
- 1 cup dairy sour cream
- 2 teaspoons sugar
- ¼ teaspoon ground ginger
- dash salt

Dissolve gelatin in boiling water. Add berries, stirring occasionally until thawed. Stir in pineapple, bananas and pecans. Pour into a 9x13-inch glass dish. Chill until firm (about 5 to 6 hours). Top with sour cream, sugar, ginger and dash of salt. Chill well. Yield: 8 servings.

**Cheryl Harris,
Texas Ranger
Association Foundation**

This recipe was given to me nearly 20 years ago by one of my best friends, Nina Loftis, when we were just kids - trying to raise kids! My children, Roxanne and Brandi, and Nina's, Chris and Brooke, say this is their favorite recipe.

PRETZEL SALAD

- 1½ sticks margarine
- 2⅔ cups coarsely crushed pretzels
- 8 ounces cream cheese
- 1 cup sugar
- 1 package whipped topping mix
- 2 cups pineapple juice
- 2 small packages strawberry Jello
- 20 ounces frozen strawberries

Melt margarine in 9x12x2-inch baking pan. Add pretzels. Mix well and bake at 400° for 10 minutes. Cool. Blend the cream cheese and sugar. Spread over pretzels. Whip the topping mix according to package directions. Spread over cheese. Heat pineapple juice, but don't boil. Add Jello, stirring well. Add strawberries to Jello mixture and chill until slightly set. Pour over layers in pan. Chill.

Anonymous Texas Ranger

STRAWBERRY SALAD

- 1 large package strawberry Jello
- 2 packages frozen strawberries
- 1 (16 ounce) package sour cream
- 1 small can crushed pineapple
- 2 bananas
- ½ cup chopped pecans

Dissolve Jello in 2 cups water. Add strawberries and pineapple and pecans and bananas. Pour ½ of mixture into a 9x13-inch pan and let set. Spread sour cream over set Jello mixture and add remaining Jello mixture. Let set. Cut in squares and serve on lettuce.

Joe Davis, retired Ranger, and wife Lila

FALL SALAD

- 8 cups torn salad greens, chilled
- 1 cup diced red apple
- 1 cup diagonally sliced celery
- ⅔ cup oil
- 1 cup vinegar
- 1 teaspoon sugar
- ½ teaspoon salt
- ⅛ teaspoon black pepper
- ¼ cup crumbled blue cheese
- 2 cups chopped nuts

Combine greens, apples and celery. Shake together oil, vinegar, sugar, salt and pepper. Pour over salad. Add cheese and toss lightly. Garnish with nuts.

Charles Schreiner III, and wife Karol

CHICKEN TORTILLA SOUP

Boil 4 large chicken breasts, one large chopped onion, one bay leaf and one crushed garlic clove until chicken is done. Remove bay leaf. Remove chicken and tear in small pieces. Leave large amount of broth. You may add bullion cube if desired. Add to broth one large can chopped chilies, three tablespoons chili powder, one can pinto beans, one can whole kernel corn, 2 teaspoons basil, 2 cans diced tomatoes. Boil and serve. When in bowl crush in large pieces tortilla chips.

Edith Kidd
Texas Ranger
Association Foundation
Member

TACO SOUP

- 2 pounds ground beef
- 1 chopped onion
- 1 package taco seasoning
- 1 package dry ranch dressing mix
- garlic powder
- 1 can cut-up tomatoes
- 1 can drained yellow hominy
- 1 can tomatoes and green chilies
- 1 can pinto beans
- 1 can light kidney beans

Brown meat and onion in Dutch oven. Drain. Add all other ingredients. Cook for 15 to 20 minutes on medium to low heat until heated through. Can be doubled and freezes well. Serves 6 to 8.

Buzz Dulick, Texas Ranger Association Foundation, and wife Judy

Substitute ground turkey meat for ground beef and jalapeño pinto beans for more spice.

This recipe was given to my daughter by her friend Terry Irby of Ft. Worth.

FRED'S TACO SOUP

- 2 pounds ground beef
- 2 cans yellow & white hominy
- 1 can jalapeño Ranch Style beans
- 1 can pinto beans
- 2 cans kidney beans
- 2 cans chopped, stewed tomatoes
- 1 can tomatoes and green chilies
- 2 cups water
- 1 package dry ranch dressing mix

Brown meat and drain. Add all other ingredients. Heat for 20 to 30 minutes. Serve with tostado chips or cornbread.

Sergeant Fred Cummings, Company F, and wife Connie

COMPANY B CHILI

Brown 6 pounds coarse ground chuck or rump roast in an iron skillet. Place browned meat in a large pot over low heat. Add one large can of tomato sauce with green chilies, one small bottle Gebhardt's chili powder, one large chopped onion, one teaspoon cumin, two cloves chopped garlic or garlic powder. Salt to taste. Stir well. Add water to cover meat. Adjust heat to bring to boil then lower temperature to simmer about two hours. Stir occasionally.

Before serving, mix masa in hot water and mix well. Add to chili to thicken as desired. More or less spices may be used to suit taste. Serve steaming hot in preheated bowls with chips or crackers. This is excellent served over scrambled eggs with hot biscuits for breakfast or over tamales and enchiladas.

Sgt. Stuart Dowell, retired Ranger

POTATO CHEESE SOUP

4 cubes beef bouillon
6 cups boiling water
1 small jar pasteurized processed cheese spread
1 package frozen hash-brown potatoes
garlic salt
celery salt
1 grated carrot

Dissolve bouillon cubes in boiling water. Add remaining ingredients. Bring to a boil and simmer until potatoes are tender.

Sergeant Danny Rhea,
Company B,
and wife Sue

CAULDO

Fill a 1½- to 2-gallon pot ⅔ full of water. Place in 6 to 8 meaty soup bones, 8 to 10 cloves of garlic, peeled and cut in half, salt, pepper and 2 bunches chopped cilantro. Boil for 45 minutes to 1 hour. Add 2 to 3 pounds stew meat, new potatoes (whole in skin), diced carrots (½-inch or so), turnips cut in half with skin, zucchini squash, corn on the cob quartered about 2 inches long, celery cut into 2-inch long cubes, and 1 to 2 heads of cabbage cut in half or quarters. Cook until cabbage is done (about 15 minutes). Serve in large bowls with corn or flour tortillas. Squeeze lime into soup when serving for additional flavor.

Sergeant H. Joaquin Jackson,
Company E

I got this recipe from a Mexican lady who ran a cafe I frequented out in Zavala, Co., in 1969. She really did know how to cook!

BROCCOLI CHEESE SOUP

3 carrots
3 ribs celery
3 green onions
1 box chopped broccoli
2 tablespoons butter
2 cans chicken broth
2 cans potato soup
1 pound cubed pasteurized process cheese spread

Peel carrots. Slice carrots, celery and onion into ¼-inch slices. Add chopped broccoli and sauté in butter. To this mixture add undiluted chicken broth and undiluted potato soup. Simmer on low flame until vegetables are thoroughly cooked; soft but not mushy. Add cubed cheese and simmer until completely melted and soup is hot. Stir as needed.

Sergeant W. R. "Bill" Gerth,
Company C,
and wife Dixie

CHEESE CHOWDER

1 cup shredded carrots
1 cup chopped celery
1½ cups water
½ cup chopped onion
6 tablespoons margarine
½ cup flour
4 cups milk
3½ cups chicken broth
2 pounds pasteurized process cheese spread
3 cups shredded Cheddar cheese

Cook carrots and celery in water until tender. Do not drain! Cook onions in margarine until tender. Stir in flour. Add milk. Cook and stir until thick. Add chicken broth, cheese and vegetables (with liquid). Stir over low heat until cheese melts.

Sergeant Kyle Dean,
Company B

STEWED STEW

Put 1 pound of stew meat in a large pot. Peel and cut up 1 pound potatoes. Peel 2 carrots. Add to meat. Pour in 2 gallons whiskey, 1 quart MILLER LITE BEER and 1 pint of gin. Cook for 3 hours. Dump out first 3 ingredients and drink the gravy.

Captain Jack Dean,
Company D,
and wife Janie

OYSTER STEW

- 2 tablespoons all-purpose flour
- 1½ teaspoons salt
- 1 teaspoon Worcestershire sauce
- dash hot pepper sauce
- 2 tablespoons water
- 1 pint undrained, shucked oysters
- ¼ cup butter or margarine
- 1 quart scalded milk

Blend flour, salt, sauces and water in a 3-quart soup kettle. Add oysters and butter. Simmer on very low heat, stirring gently, for 3 to 4 minutes till edges of oysters curl. Add milk; remove from heat and cover. Let stand 15 minutes, reheat briefly. Top servings with pats of butter. Serves 4 or 5.

Gaines de Graffenried,
Late Curator Texas
Ranger Museum And
Hall Of Fame

Submitted by his son, Tommy de Graffenried.

TEXAS COWBOY STEW

- 6 slices bacon
- 1 cup sliced onion
- ½ cup chopped bell pepper
- 1½ pounds lean ground beef
- 1 clove garlic, crushed
- 1 teaspoon salt
- ¼ teaspoon black pepper
- 1 tablespoon chili powder
- 2 large cans tomatoes
- 2 cups cubed potatoes
- 1 can corn

Fry bacon, remove from skillet. Sauté onions and bell pepper in bacon drippings. Add ground beef and garlic. Brown together and simmer 30 minutes. Add salt, pepper, chili powder, tomatoes and potatoes. Cook on low heat in electric skillet until potatoes are done. Add corn and simmer 10 minutes. When stew is done, crumble bacon and add.

Sergeant Jim Gillespie,
Company C

SON OF A GUN STEW

- 1 pound steak
- 1 pound heart
- ½ pound sweetbreads
- 1½ pounds liver
- ½ pound kidney
- ½ pound brains (optional)
- ½ pound marrowgut (optional)
- 2½ pounds ground beef
- 5 medium onions
- 6 medium potatoes
- 2 pods garlic
- 10 medium tomatoes
- 2 packages English peas
- 4 bell peppers
- salt & pepper

Cut meat into bite sized pieces, about the size of a thumb joint. Brown meats in big black pot (if available). Cover with water, add vegetables and cook slowly all day. Add one can of beer midway through. Add additional water if necessary. Serves 16 to 20.

Walter A. "Bob" Werner, Retired, and wife Jeanne

For hot stew add jalapeños, chili pequin and/or banana peppers. May use liver, heart and steak from venison for a different flavored stew.

Along with this recipe, Bob sent me to following note:

Dear Johnny,
I enclosed this one just for the "hell" of it. Among my friends, I call it the "Henry Lee Lucas Special" However, it does make a good stew and any ingredient is optional.

Bob

ELEPHANT STEW

Cut 1 medium elephant into small bite-sized pieces. This will take about two months. Keep the trunk! You'll need something to store the pieces in. Add enough brown gravy to cover. Cook over a kerosene fire for about 4 weeks at 465 degrees. Add salt and pepper to taste. This will serve about 38,000 people. If more are expected, two rabbits may be added to the pot, but do this only if necessary. Most people do not like hare in their stew.

Captain Jack Dean, Company D, and wife Janie

Sergeant Jim Gillespie, Company C

Genn Krueger, and wife Jackie

MEXICAN STEW

- **1½ pounds ground beef**
- **chopped onions**
- **3 cans Mexican stewed tomatoes**
- **1 can Ranch Style beans (do not drain)**
- **1 can jalapeño pinto beans (do not drain)**
- **1 can yellow hominy (do not drain)**
- **1 package dry ranch dressing mix**

Brown meat with onions (as many as you like). Drain meat and place in a stew pot. Add tomatoes, beans and hominy; do not drain cans. Add dressing mix. Mix and heat until very hot. Great with cornbread.

Glenn Krueger, and wife Jackie

This recipe was given to me by Mrs. Lloyd (Pat) Hemphill of Fredericksburg. It is very good when serving a crowd.

TEXAS RANGER STEW

- 1 (28 ounce) can peeled whole tomatoes, crushed
- 2 (6 to 8 ounce) cans sliced mushrooms
- 1 can beef broth
- 2 soup cans of water
- ¼ cup catsup
- 2 tablespoons Worcestershire sauce
- 1 small chopped onion
- 1½ teaspoons salt
- ½ teaspoon ground thyme
- ⅛ teaspoon pepper
- 1½ pounds lean hamburger
- 1 cup quick cooking rice

Brown meat and onion, drain fat. Add tomatoes, broth, water, catsup, sauce, salt, thyme, pepper and mushrooms. Bring to a boil. Reduce heat and simmer uncovered for 5 minutes. Stir in rice, cover and set aside for 5 minutes. Wonderful with cornbread.

Sgt. Brantley Foster, Company B, and wife Suzanne

HOT SAUCE

- 1 can chopped green chilies
- ½ dozen fresh jalapeño peppers
- ½ onion
- 1 pod fresh garlic
- 1 can stewed tomatoes
- pinch of salt

Place all items into a blender on chop until a thick sauce. Has plenty of kick.

C. J. "Buster" Collins, Company E

JOHN'S BARBECUE SAUCE

- 1 gallon ketchup
- 1 quart mustard
- ½ gallon water
- ¼ ounce hot pepper sauce
- 32 ounces Worcestershire sauce
- 6 ounces lemon juice
- 6 ounces sugar
- ½ ounce salt
- 1 teaspoon black pepper

Mix all ingredients together. Fun to experiment with by adding garlic powder, onion flakes or celery seeds.

John Dendy, Retired, and wife Vineta

HEADQUARTERS BARBECUE SAUCE

- 1 cup peanut oil
- 3 medium onions, chopped
- 1 cup chopped bell pepper
- 1 cup chopped celery
- 1 cup chopped parsley
- 2 tablespoons minced garlic
- 3 cups steak sauce
- 3 cups ketchup
- 1 cup Southern Comfort

In large pan heat oil to hot. Add onion, bell pepper and celery. Mix well. Add parsley, garlic, steak sauce, ketchup and Southern Comfort. Stir after each addition. Cover and simmer for 2 to 3 hours.

Sergeant L. R. "Rocky" Wardlow, Headquarters Company

This recipe is endorsed by Bastrop Police Chief Ronnie Duncan, who is a world renowned brisket cooker and legend in his own mind. He really does cook a good brisket though!

EASY BARBECUE SAUCE

- 6 cups water
- 28 ounces ketchup
- 1¼ cups sugar
- 1 tablespoon paprika
- 2 tablespoons garlic powder
- ½ cup vinegar
- ½ cup Worcestershire sauce
- dash Liquid Smoke
- 2 medium onions, chopped
- ½ lemon

Mix water, ketchup, sugar, paprika, garlic powder, vinegar, Worcestershire sauce and liquid smoke in a heavy pan. Bring to a boil. Lower heat and simmer 1 to 2 hours or until reduced and beginning to thicken. Add the onions and the juice of the lemon half, then drop in the lemon rind. Simmer another 45 minutes, stirring occasionally. Strain before use. Yield: Makes about 1 quart.

Bill Gunn, Retired, and wife Sugar

PICO DE GALLO

3 cups chopped onions
3 cups chopped, firm pink tomatoes
2 chopped avocados
1-2 teaspoons finely chopped jalapeño peppers
3 tablespoons finely chopped cilantro
2 juiced limes
garlic salt
coarse ground black pepper

Combine all ingredients and mix well. Refrigerate. Serve with fajitas, tortilla chips or Mexican egg dishes.

Bill Gunn, Retired, and wife Sugar

TOMATO PICO DE GALLO

3 large tomatoes
6 large green tomatoes
¼ pod garlic
3 jalapeño peppers
5 banana peppers
1 large onion
2 tablespoons salt

Quarter red and green tomatoes. Mince garlic. Cut peppers into quarters. Chop onion. Blend all ingredients in a blender until they are a liquid. Taste the liquid for fire control and cook it in a pot until it meets your thickness test. Pour the green concoction into boiled jars and seal with a hot lid. Those folks that like red pepper sauce can sure use more red tomatoes than green ones. There are no preservatives in this old recipe so don't make a washtub full of this wonderful stuff.

Sergeant John Aycock, Company F, and wife Estelle

CHERRY SAUCE

For a good cherry sauce, mix ¼ cup brandy and ½ cup chopped pecans into a small jar of cherry preserves. Heat and serve over ice cream.

John Barron Harris,
Texas Ranger
Association Foundation,
and wife Cheryl

MAPLE SAUCE

Heat maple syrup. Add 1 tablespoon butter and ½ cup toasted pecans. Serve over pound cake or ice cream.

John Barron Harris,
Texas Ranger
Association Foundation,
and wife Cheryl

POPPY SEED DRESSING

⅔ cup champagne or white wine vinegar
2 cups oil
1½ cups sugar
2 teaspoons dry mustard
3 tablespoons onion juice
3 tablespoons poppy seed
2 teaspoons salt

With a mixer on very slow speed, add vinegar to oil one spoon at a time to make mixture very creamy. Slowly add other ingredients. Serve over fresh fruit cut in bite size pieces. Use plenty of Fruit Fresh so fruit will remain fresh. Store dressing in refrigerator and serve over fruit. Yield: Makes approximately ¾ quart of dressing.

Bill Gunn, Retired,
and wife Sugar

Ranger camp at Menard, Texas.

Donkey to go on a scout in rough country.

★ ★ ★ ★

Sidelines

Photograph courtesy of Bill Gunn Collection

Rangers on a scout.

BILL WILSON

As a young man Bill Wilson was an outstanding athlete. He played football in high school and also basketball, and he made all state in football in high school on a team that only won one game out of twelve. In later life he was an outstanding man, well liked, highly respected and beloved by everyone who knew him. Bill was a very compassionate leader and was always concerned about the well being of the people who worked for him as well as their families. He commanded the respect of everyone, all of his contemporaries and the people that worked under him. He went to the University of Texas on a football scholarship and finished the season just in time to go to the nineteenth Highway Patrol school. This is where he began his career in law enforcement and he established quite a reputation as a law man. Always a sportsman, he loved football, basketball, hunting and fishing. One of the last things he did just before he passed away was to ask Bob Mitchell and Jack Dean to go on one last fishing trip with him. He died about two weeks after this trip. He had one daughter and two grandchildren of which he was very proud, and I know they are proud of him.

Bill Wilson was fearless in any kind of confrontation. He always expected anyone who worked for him to be the first up in any situation. He wanted his company to be the first to go to the door or do whatever might be necessary in a confrontation of any kind. There was one case where a suspect had taken refuge in his home and he was firing at the officers who were trying to arrest him. A number of rangers were called in. This was down in Guadalupe county close to McQueen. Bill and Jim Reynolds out of Austin, Clint Peoples, Wallace Miller and some others were all there surrounding the house. They shot the house full of gas, but they never could subdue the man. Every time they started in, he began to shoot again. They couldn't figure out how he was able to repel the gas. Bill slipped around to the back door and slipped in. When he did, he heard water running. As he watched the man was in the shower with the water running on his head. Consequently the gas was not bothering him. He would step out every few minutes and take another couple of shots and then get back in the shower. Bill waited for an opportunity and grabbed him out of the shower and dragged him out the back door.

After Bill got extremely sick and was unable to walk around the golf course, there were a number of his friends that chipped in and bought him a golf cart so he could continue to play golf which he loved very much. The golf cart was painted burnt orange and white, the University of Texas colors. Bill was an outstanding man well loved by all his friends and the people who worked for him. Everyone he knew held him in high regard.

QUANAH PARKER

Quanah Parker was the son of a captured white woman named Cynthia Ann Parker and Chief Peta Nacoona. At the battle of Pease River in 1860, Peta Nacoona was killed by Captain Sul Ross. Cynthia Ann was returned to her white family. She had forgotten how to speak English and never re-adapted to the white man's way of life. She grieved herself to death about ten years later.

As a young man, Quanah Parker was among the Comanches who raided along the Llamo Estacado in the areas of Fort Richardson, Fort Belknap, Fort Bliss, Fort Stockton and Fort Griffin. In a battle on the Red River, Quanah Parker was chosen as leader of the tribe after the death of Chief Bear's Ear. In August of 1871, General Ranald S. Mackenzie set out to punish the Comanche. Quanah Parker and a group of braves stole all of the general's horses.

When Quanah Parker was finally subdued by the Texas Rangers, they told him he would have to tell his wives that he couldn't keep but one of them. His answer was,

"You tell 'em!"

CHILI BEANS

- 2 pounds washed pinto beans
- 1 pound chopped bacon
- 2 onions, chopped
- 2 cans tomato sauce
- 1 small can chopped green chilies
- ⅓ cup Worcestershire sauce
- ¾ cup brown sugar
- 2 tablespoons garlic powder
- 4 tablespoons chili powder
- 1 tablespoon ground cumin
- 1 tablespoon black pepper
- ¼ cup salt

Combine all ingredients in Dutch oven. Cover with water. Cook with the lid on at 250° overnight or 12 hours. Add water when needed.

Sergeant Jim Gillespie,
Company C

May add 1 pound or more of cooked ground beef for a meat dish.

DIXIE'S HOT PINTO BEANS

- 2 pounds pinto beans
- 2 teaspoons salt
- 2 large diced onions
- 4 cloves garlic
- 1 bunch chopped green onion
- 1 can tomatoes
- 1 can tomatoes and green chilies
- 2 teaspoons chili powder

Soak beans overnight in cold water. Drain and wash. Cover with fresh water. Add salt and cook over moderate heat for 1 hour. Add hot water if necessary. Add remaining ingredients. Simmer over low heat for 1½ hours.

Sergeant W. R. "Bill" Gerth,
Company C,
and wife Dixie

PINTO BEANS

- 2 pounds pinto beans
- 1½ medium chopped onions
- ½ pound bacon

Place all ingredients in a pot with water to soak overnight. Boil till done at about 400°. Season to taste with garlic salt, coarse ground black pepper or chili powder.

Bill Gunn, Retired,
and wife Sugar

While stationed in Brownwood information came to me and a DPS Narcotics officer of local drug dealing. The Narcotics officer and his "compadres" had set up a "buy-bust" deal at the local airport and I was asked to assist.

All officers involved had several meetings whereby assignments were made after a working plan was organized. The day came to put the plan in operation. The informant (a DPS Narcotics officer) and another NARC were to fly into Brownwood airport in a DPS aircraft and the drug dealer was to bring the drugs to the aircraft where the "buy-bust" was to be made. One of the officers at the aircraft was to signal other officers by taking off his cap as soon as they saw the drugs.

All officers involved drove to the airport in a van and each officer took his assigned place to await the arrival of the dealer or dealers. Two Brown County Sheriff's officers in separate cars were to block the only road leading to the airport as soon as they were notified the signal had been given. My station was sitting in an aircraft near the gate to the airport apron. No one knew how many "dealers" would arrive or in what type vehicle.

After a short waiting period, with all officers at their assigned stations, a car drove up to the gate with three males aboard. Another five minute wait and one of the passengers got out of the car, looked all around, then took a briefcase out of the car and began walking toward the DPS aircraft. The driver of the car pulled forward and to the left facing back toward the highway, apparently for a fast "get-away". That move placed the back of the car to me about 50 feet away. The "crook" with the drugs arrived at the DPS aircraft and after a few minutes the cap came off. Things began to happen very quickly at this point.

I got out of the aircraft I was hiding in and began walking toward the suspects' car. The suspects, I noticed, were both looking toward the DPS aircraft. I then saw the driver look back and when he saw me walking toward them he threw the car in gear and sped away, squealing tires and throwing gravel.

The Sheriff's officers were notified (by radio) to block the road just as I noticed one of the Sheriff's Office cars approaching, meeting the "crooks" car. I then heard two or three shots as I saw the Sheriff's Office unit make a fast "U" turn in pursuit. I did not know if the shots were fired by the deputy or by the crooks. There was a lot of radio chatter at this point and I could not understand all the transmissions. I did hear that the crooks turned north on the highway and a very short time later that someone "wrecked out", not knowing if it was the crooks or the officer. The Sheriff's officers would not or could not answer the radio calls to them.

I became afraid that the officers had wrecked and the crooks were getting away. With no pursuit vehicle available I felt helpless a few seconds until a friend of mine standing there, a seasoned pilot, asked me if I wanted an airplane. That question did not need an answer. He and I immediately ran for one of his airplanes, did not even take the time to fasten seat belts, and became airborne just off the taxi-way using only a very short part of the runway. We made a very low left turn and headed north along the highway. About five miles from the airport we observed two Sheriff's units and another vehicle at odd angles in a bar ditch at an intersecting gravel road.

Not being able to detect what exactly was happening on the ground the pilot asked me if I wanted to land. I gave an affirmative nod, noting there was little or no highway traffic, and we landed on the road and taxied up to the Sheriff's Office units. As I ran up to the three cars it was evident that the bad guys had crashed and the two Sheriff's officers had the situation well in hand. A .38 caliber pistol was found on the floorboard of the suspect's car. The two suspects were handcuffed and searched. The next problem was getting back in the air.

I radioed for assistance to block the highway at both ends so we might safely get back into the air. I was advised by radio that the north and south had officers stopping any traffic and we began our take-off run, headed south. I then noticed a highline across the road and a truck-tractor-trailer rig headed toward us that did not stop for the flagging officer. I asked the pilot if we were going over or under the highline. He said "under". We had to move to the right to avoid the truck, narrowly missed several mailboxes with the right wing, missed the truck, went under the highline and became airborne once again. The pilot, a retired US Air Force pilot, Pete Michaud, looked at me and stated his favorite saying, "Well we cheated death one more time." God bless Pete, my friend.

Norman Autrey, Retired

BEAN POT

1 chopped green pepper
1 chopped onion
1/8 teaspoon garlic powder
1/2 cup ketchup
1/4 teaspoon black pepper
1 teaspoon dry mustard
3 tablespoons brown sugar
1 can pork & beans
1 can green Lima beans
1 can kidney beans

Fry green pepper and onion in a little butter or bacon grease until limp. Add garlic powder, ketchup, pepper, mustard and brown sugar. Stir in all beans. Mix well and simmer for 30 minutes or bake uncovered in oven 45 minutes at 325°.

Sergeant Morgan L. Miller, Company D, and wife Ann

COUNTRY POTATOES

2 pounds frozen hash-brown potatoes
1 stick margarine
1 can cream of chicken soup
2 cups grated Cheddar cheese
1/2 cup chopped green onion
1 cup sour cream
2 tablespoons melted margarine
1 cup crushed corn flakes

Mix first 6 ingredients in large bowl. Butter large baking dish. Pour mixture into dish. Mix melted margarine and corn flakes. Put on top and bake at 350° for 45 minutes.

Capt. Bob Prince, Retired

GUNN'S POTATOES

5 medium potatoes
1 stick margarine
1/2 cup water
1 package onion soup mix

Brush potatoes clean and dice thin. Cut margarine into pieces. Mix all ingredients together in a skillet and cook on medium heat until potatoes are soft. Season to taste with garlic salt, coarse ground black pepper and paprika.

Bill Gunn, Retired, and wife Sugar

CHEESE TATERS

- 1 pound thawed hash-brown potatoes
- ½ cup sour cream
- ½ can cream of chicken soup
- 6 ounces grated Cheddar cheese
- ½ stick melted margarine
- ¼ cup chopped onion
- salt & pepper
- corn flakes

Place the hash-brown potatoes in 2-quart casserole dish. In large bowl combine the sour cream, soup, cheese, margarine and onion. Salt & pepper to taste. Pour over potatoes and mix together. Crumble some corn flakes on top of the mixture and drizzle with melted butter if desired. Bake at 350° for 45 minutes. For larger families just double the recipe. Potatoes are just as good warmed up after they have been frozen.

Sergeant John Aycock,
Company F,
and wife Estelle

DEPRESSION POTATOES

- 2 medium potatoes, cubed
- 1 medium onion, diced
- handful sliced fresh okra
- cornmeal

Mix all ingredients together. Coat with cornmeal. You may want to moisten the ingredients if you like a thicker coating. Fry in hot fat in a skillet until golden brown and crispy. Drain well.

Sergeant John Aycock,
Company F,
and wife Estelle

This recipe was passed down to us from someone who lived through the depression.

COWBOY POTATOES

- 4-5 medium potatoes
- 1 medium onion
- 1 bell pepper
- black pepper
- garlic salt
- 1 can cream of mushroom soup
- 1 can cream of celery soup
- jalapeño peppers

Cut potatoes into ½-inch cubes. Cut onion and bell pepper the same or slightly smaller. Place in large bowl and stir to mix well. Add pepper and garlic salt to taste. Add undiluted soup. Stir in jalapeños if desired. Mix well. Put into large baking dish. Cover with foil and cook at about 350° for 1¼ hours or until potatoes are tender. Sprinkle Cheddar cheese on top and put back into oven without covering just long enough to melt the cheese.

Marrie Garcia,
Company B,
and husband Robert

SINFUL POTATOES

- 2 pounds thawed hash-brown potatoes
- 1 stick melted margarine
- 1 teaspoon salt
- ⅛ teaspoon black pepper
- 2 cups shredded Cheddar cheese
- 1 can cream of mushroom soup
- 2 cups sour cream
- ½ cup chopped onion

Grease well a 9x13-inch baking pan. In a large bowl combine all ingredients. Mix well and pour into pan. If desired, sprinkle unseasoned breadcrumbs on top. Bake for 1 hour at 350°.

Sergeant Kyle Dean,
Company B

POTATO LATKES

- 4 large potatoes
- 1 medium onion
- 1 teaspoon salt
- 3 tablespoons flour
- ½ teaspoon baking powder
- 2 eggs, beaten

Grate raw potatoes that have been washed and pared. Grate the onion and add it to the potatoes. Mix together salt, flour and baking powder. Add eggs and flour mixture to potatoes. Beat all ingredients well into a smooth batter. If the batter seems too watery, add a little more flour. Drop by tablespoonfuls into hot oil in a heavy frying pan. The oil must be deep enough to almost cover the cake. Brown on one side, and with pancake turner, turn to brown on other side. Drain on absorbent paper. Serve piping hot. Delicious when served with applesauce (some say sour cream).

Captain Jack Dean,
Company D,
and wife Janie

SWEET POTATO CASSEROLE

- 3 large sweet potatoes
- ½ cup butter
- 2 eggs
- ⅓ cup evaporated milk
- ¾ cup sugar
- 1 teaspoon vanilla
- ¾ cup brown sugar
- ⅔ cup melted butter
- 1 cup chopped pecans

Bake sweet potatoes, peel and mash. Add ½ cup butter, eggs, milk, sugar and vanilla. Mix with mixer and pour into greased casserole. For topping, mix together brown sugar, ⅔ cup butter and pecans. Spread over potato mixture. Bake at 350° for 35 to 40 minutes. Let cool for 15 to 20 minutes before serving.

Sergeant Jesse Priest, Retired

YUMMY YAMS

- 3 cups cooked, mashed yams
- 1½ cups sugar
- ¾ stick margarine
- 1 cup evaporated milk
- 3 beaten eggs
- ½ teaspoon nutmeg
- ½ teaspoon salt
- ½ teaspoon cinnamon
- 1 teaspoon vanilla
- ¾ stick melted margarine
- ½ cup brown sugar
- ½ cup chopped pecans
- 1 cup crushed corn flakes

Mix together yams, sugar, ¾ stick of margarine, milk, eggs, nutmeg, salt, cinnamon and vanilla. Put in 8x8x2-inch uncovered dish. Bake at 425° for 15 minutes. Mix together melted margarine, brown sugar, pecans and corn flakes. Place on top of mixture in oven. Reduce heat to 400° and bake an additional 15 minutes.

Capt. Bob Prince, Retired

GRILLED CORN-ON-THE-COB

Use medium sized ears of corn. Open the outer husks of corn and remove the silk. Add pats of butter to corn. Replace the husks and wrap closely in aluminum foil. Place in hot coals on grill and cook for 10 to 20 minutes. Remove from husks. Season with butter, salt and pepper. Serve while hot.

John Barron Harris,
Texas Ranger
Association Foundation,
and wife Cheryl

CORN DISH

- 16 ounces cream cheese
- 1 stick margarine
- 1 can chopped green chilies
- 4 cans corn, drained

Melt cream cheese and butter in microwave until soft. Add chilies and corn. Bake at 300° for 30 to 45 minutes.

Capt. Bob Prince, Retired

KAROL'S CORN CASSEROLE

4 eggs, beaten
1 cup oil
1 package jalapeño cornbread mix
½ cup grated Cheddar cheese
½ cup cream cheese
1 can cream style corn
1 can whole kernel corn
chopped onion (optional)

Mix together the eggs, oil and cornbread mix. Stir in the cheese, corn and onion. Pour into casserole dish. Bake 45 minutes at 400°.

**Charles Schreiner III,
and wife Karol**

CORN CASSEROLE

¼ cup butter
¼ cup chopped onion
¼ cup chopped celery
¼ cup chopped green pepper
1 cup milk
2 tablespoons flour
1 teaspoon salt
¼ teaspoon paprika
1 large can corn
2 tablespoons parsley
2 well beaten eggs

Melt butter. Add onion, celery and green pepper. Cook until soft. Blend in milk, flour, salt and paprika. Heat until it bubbles, bring rapidly to a boil. Cook 2 minutes. Mix in corn and parsley. Remove from heat and add eggs. Turn into buttered casserole dish and bake at 350° for 35 minutes.

**Bill Gunn, Retired,
and wife Sugar**

CORN CASSEROLE SOUFFLÉ

2 (16½ ounce) cans of yellow cream corn
1 (4 ounce) can chopped green chilies (drained)
½ cup chopped onion
1 cup milk
2 eggs (lightly beaten)
1 cup yellow cornmeal
1½ teaspoons garlic salt
½ teaspoon baking soda

Combine first 6 ingredients in a large bowl. Combine cornmeal, garlic salt and baking soda. Stir into corn mixture and pour into a greased 11x17½-inch baking dish. Bake at 350° approximately 50 minutes

**Adrienne Moorhead
Texas Ranger
Association Foundation
Member**

SPICY MEXICAN CORN

- 8 ounces picante sauce
- 16 ounces frozen corn
- ½ cup shredded mozzarella cheese

Drain picante sauce, reserving liquid. Measure reserved liquid, adding water if necessary to measure ½ cup. Combine liquid and corn in saucepan. Cook uncovered over medium heat, stirring occasionally, about 5 minutes or until tender. Pour in serving bowl. Stir in picante and sprinkle with cheese.

Bill Gunn, Retired,
and wife Sugar

CALABACITAS

- 1 medium onion
- 1 clove garlic
- 4 medium size zucchini
- 2 tablespoons oil
- 1 (12 ounce) can niblet corn, drained
- 1 (4 ounce) can diced green chilies
- salt
- ½ cup grated Cheddar or Monterey Jack cheese (optional)

In large heavy skillet sauté onion, garlic and sliced zucchini in oil. Discard garlic. Mix in corn, chilies and salt to taste. Cover and heat through. Mix in cheese, warm just to melt, then serve. Makes 4 servings.

John Barron Harris,
Texas Ranger
Association Foundation,
and wife Cheryl

MIKE'S HOMINY CASSEROLE

- 1 stick margarine
- 3 cans hominy
- 1 can cream of celery soup
- 1 can milk
- 4 ounces cubed cream cheese
- breadcrumbs
- nuts

Melt margarine in casserole dish. Add hominy. Stir in soup and milk. Stir in cheese. Garnish with crumbs and nuts. Salt to taste. Bake uncovered at 350° until brown on top.

Captain Carl Weathers,
Company C,
and wife Mickey

This recipe came from Etta Connell, wife of Bob Connell, Retired, of Company F.

HOMINY CASSEROLE

- 2 cans drained, washed hominy
- 1 can tomatoes
- 1 pound pasteurized process cheese spread

In 1½- or 2-quart greased casserole, layer one can of hominy. Cover evenly with ½ can tomatoes. Top with thinly sliced pieces of cheese. Repeat procedure for second layer. Be sure cheese on top layer completely covers hominy and tomatoes. Bake at 350° for approximately 30 minutes or until cheese is melted evenly on top and casserole is thoroughly heated.

Sergeant W. R. "Bill" Gerth,
Company C,
and wife Dixie

BOB'S HOMINY CASSEROLE

- 1 stick margarine
- 3 cans yellow hominy
- 1 can cream of celery soup
- 1 soup can evaporated milk
- ½ teaspoon salt
- 4 ounces cubed cream cheese
- ¼ cup cracker crumbs
- ¼ cup crumbled pecans

Melt margarine in casserole. Add hominy. Stir in soup, milk, and salt. Stir in cream cheese. Garnish with crumbs and nuts. Bake uncovered at 350° till brown on top, about 30 minutes.

Bob Connell, Retired,
and wife Etta

This recipe is for the East Texas soul food crowd.

COPPER PENNY CARROTS

- 2 cans sliced carrots, drained
- 1 chopped bell pepper
- 1 chopped onion
- 1 cup sugar
- ½ cup oil
- 1 can tomato soup
- 1 teaspoon Worcestershire sauce
- ¾ cup vinegar
- 1 teaspoon mustard

In a saucepan, combine sugar, oil, undiluted soup, Worcestershire sauce, vinegar and mustard. Bring to a boil. Combine carrots, bell pepper and onion in a bowl. Pour sauce over top. Mix well. Refrigerate until ready to serve.

Cathy Brumbalow
Office Manager
Harris Farms

BROCCOLI RICE CASSEROLE

- 2 cups cooked rice
- ½ cup celery
- ½ cup onions
- ½ stick Oleo
- ½ cup milk
- 1 can cream of mushroom soup
- 1 box frozen broccoli, cooked, cooled and drained
- 1 small jar Cheese Whiz
- salt and pepper

Sauté celery and onion in oleo, Add milk, soup, cooked broccoli, and Cheese Whiz. Stir in rice. Bake at 350° for 30 minutes.

Lt. Earl R. Pearson, Company F
and wife Patricia

GREENS & POT LIKKER

- ½ pound salt pork
- 1 quart water
- 4 quarts turnip greens
- salt & pepper

Start salt pork in cold water. Cook 50 minutes. Add washed and chopped turnip greens to pork and cook 1 hour (until water is cooked down). Season to taste.

Sergeant Jim Gillespie,
Company C

POKE SALET

- 1 gallon washed poke salet greens
- wild onions or 1 bunch fresh green onions
- 16 cups water, divided
- salt
- pepper
- 6 eggs
- 3 tablespoons cream
- 4 tablespoons bacon drippings

Poke salet grows wild. Greens that the early settlers, Indians and pioneers ate along the trail and in their homes in the early spring, after a hard winter of meat and potatoes. Pick early when it first starts to come out - young shoots and tender leaves are the best. Wash carefully 3 or 4 times to make sure leaves and shoots are clean. Place greens in a large pan with 4 cups of water. Bring to a boil for 5 minutes. Drain. Do this 2 more times, using 4 cups of fresh water each time. (This is very important! Some wild greens can be poisonous if not par-boiled 3 times.) Then place 4 cups of fresh water in the pot with the greens. Boil for 15 minutes or until tender. Drain. In a large iron skillet over medium heat, combine bacon drippings, poke salet greens, chopped onions, salt and pepper. Cook until water disappears. Stir occasionally to keep from sticking. Beat eggs with cream, salt and pepper until foamy. Pour into skillet with poke salet and stir until eggs are done.

Cheryl Harris,
Texas Ranger
Association Foundation

When we were little my dad, Barney Ward, used to take my brother, Dennis, and me fishing a lot in the spring. The poke salet greens grew wild and abundant along the banks of the Red River. On the way home we would gather these flavorful greens and wild onions for Dad to cook. Our mother loved these greens and it sure helped work as peace-maker after we came in the house with our muddy feet, dragging a big catfish and smellin' real fishy. Especially when she had us scheduled to do something for her that day - like mow the yard.

CORNBREAD DRESSING

1 pan cornbread
10 biscuits
½ loaf whole wheat bread
1 large onion
1½ cups celery
½ stick oleo
2 teaspoons poultry seasoning
1 teaspoon black pepper
1 teaspoon salt
2-3 raw eggs
or
2-3 boiled eggs
2 tablespoons flour

Make your pan of cornbread in an iron skillet if you have one. If not muffins are fine. We like biscuits in our dressing, so I use about 10 biscuits and about half a loaf of whole wheat bread. Mix all together - soften with some of the broth from the giblets. Sauté onion and celery in oleo (butter's better.) Add to bread mixture. Season with poultry seasoning, black pepper and salt - or salt to taste. If you like eggs in your dressing add the raw or boiled eggs (I use 3 raw eggs.) Moisten bread mixture with some of the broth from the turkey. Be sure your dressing is not stiff. Bake in greased pan for about 45 minutes, or until brown. Make gravy by adding hard-boiled eggs, the chopped liver and gizzard to some of the broth. Thin with water. Thicken by adding 2 tablespoons flour to some water and pour in the gravy slowly. (Mama's Turkey recipe on page 108).

John Barron Harris, Texas Ranger Association Foundation, and wife Cheryl

I usually cook one pan of dressing and freeze the other, as this makes a large amount. This is my mother's recipe. I have used it for years. If you like a lot of sage in your dressing, add sage. However, I only use poultry seasoning. I always cook a fat hen and use the hen's broth because it is better.

BAKED SQUASH CASSEROLE

1 medium finely chopped onion
½ cup finely diced celery
¼ cup finely diced green pepper
1 pound squash
½ cup cracker crumbs
½ stick melted margarine
1 beaten egg
2 cups grated cheese

Cook onion, celery, pepper and squash in water until tender. Drain and mash. Mix cracker crumbs, margarine and egg with squash. Pour in greased baking pan. Bake at 400° until firm and slightly brown. Cover with cheese and cover with lid to melt cheese. Serves approximately 6.

Bill Gunn, Retired, and wife Sugar

SQUASH DRESSING

1 pound sliced yellow squash
1 can cream of chicken soup
1 small jar diced pimientos
1 medium chopped onion
1 egg, beaten
2-3 cups crumbled cornbread

Cook squash in small amount of water until tender and drain. Add remaining ingredients. Mix well. Place in baking dish and cover. Bake for 45 minutes at 350°.

Captain Bob Mitchell, Retired, and wife Jerry

This dish is a light alternative to traditional dressing to be served with turkey or chicken.

SQUASH DRESSING

2 cups cornbread crumbs
2 cups cooked squash
1 chopped onion
½ stick oleo
1 can cream of chicken soup
salt and pepper

Mix bread and mashed squash - season, add onion, oleo and soup. Mix well and pour into casserole. Bake uncovered at 425° until brown. Green onions may be used instead of regular onion.

Adrienne Moorhead
Texas Ranger Association Foundation Member

SQUASH CASSEROLE

- 6 medium yellow squash
- ½ cup chopped onion
- 3 slices chopped bacon
- ¼ cup water
- salt & pepper
- 1 small carton sour cream
- ¼ box cornbread stuffing mix
- ¾ cup chicken broth

Sauté squash, onion and bacon in water until tender. Add salt, pepper and sour cream. Mix well. Prepare stuffing mix according to package directions and place half of mixture in bottom of 9x9-inch casserole dish. Pour squash mixture over stuffing and top with remainder of stuffing mix. Pour chicken broth over top and bake for approximately 30 minutes at 350°. Great served with chicken.

Jim Peters, Retired,
and wife Lydia

ZUCCHINI CASSEROLE

- 3 medium grated zucchini
- 1¼ cups herb-seasoned croutons
- ½ cup sautéed fresh mushrooms
- ½ cup chopped onion
- 2 slices cooked, crumbled bacon
- ½ cup grated Swiss cheese
- ½ cup melted butter or margarine
- 1 egg, beaten
- ½ teaspoon salt
- ¼ teaspoon black pepper
- dash garlic salt

Combine all ingredients, mixing lightly. Place in greased 1½-quart casserole and bake.

John P. Lynch, Retired,
and wife Dorothy

EGGPLANT CASSEROLE

1 eggplant
salt & pepper
flour
1 sliced green pepper
1 large sliced onion
1 large can stewed tomatoes
cheese

Slice eggplant thin and soak in cold, salty water a few minutes. Drain. Salt, pepper and flour; fry till crisp. Alternate layers with above ingredients ending with cheese on top. Bake at 350° for 30 to 45 minutes.

Anonymous Texas Ranger

GREEN TOMATO PIE

biscuit dough
sliced green tomatoes
1/8 teaspoon nutmeg
1 cup sugar
1/4 cup flour
1 cup butter
1/2 cup vinegar

Line pie pan with biscuit dough. Heap full of sliced tomatoes. Sprinkle with nutmeg, sugar and flour. Dot butter over top. Pour in vinegar before adding top crust of biscuit dough. Bake 30 minutes in moderately hot oven.

Sergeant Jim Gillespie,
Company C

CRISPY FRIED GREEN TOMATOES

green tomatoes
salt
black pepper
flour
vegetable lard

Use very firm green tomatoes, allow 2 tomatoes for each serving. Slice off top of the tomato next to the stem and also at the bottom. Slice the tomatoes 1/4-inch thick. Salt and pepper to taste. Dredge both sides in flour. Fry in a medium hot skillet with at least 1/2 inch oil covering pan. Brown both sides, being careful when turning them over. They get soft as they cook. Drain on paper towels and serve immediately while still hot!

John Barron Harris,
Texas Ranger
Association Foundation,
and wife Cheryl

MIXED VEGETABLE CASSEROLE

1 large package frozen mixed vegetables (green beans, carrots, etc.)
1 cup chopped celery
2 cups grated Cheddar cheese
1 cup mayonnaise
1 medium chopped onion
½ cup melted margarine
34 Ritz crackers, crumbled

Preheat oven to 350°. Cook vegetable and celery until tender, drain and place in a greased casserole. Combine cheese, mayonnaise and onion. Mix thoroughly and spread over vegetables. Combine margarine and crackers and sprinkle over top. Bake for 30 minutes. Serves 6 to 8.

Adrienne Moorhead
Texas Ranger
Association Foundation
Member

MEXICAN VEGGIE CASSEROLE

1½ cups corn
½ cup chopped onion
½ cup sliced green pepper
½ cup water
1 cup chopped squash
1 large chopped tomato
1 cup shredded Cheddar cheese
⅔ cup cornmeal
½ cup milk
2 beaten eggs
¾ teaspoon salt
¼ teaspoon black pepper
hot pepper sauce

In medium saucepan combine corn, onion, green pepper and water. Bring to boiling, reduce heat, cover and simmer for 5 minutes; till vegetables are crisp tender. Do not drain. Meanwhile, in large mixing bowl combine squash, tomato, ¾ cup of cheese, cornmeal, milk, eggs, salt, pepper and pepper sauce to taste. Add undrained vegetables to cornmeal mixture; mix well. Turn into greased 1½-quart casserole. Bake uncovered. Top with remaining cheese. Garnish with tomato slices and green pepper strips.

John P. Lynch, Retired,
and wife Dorothy

INSTANT MEXICAN RICE

1 can diced tomatoes and green chilies
3 cups water
3 beef bouillon cubes
salt & pepper to taste
1/8 teaspoon garlic powder
2 teaspoons chili powder
4 cups instant rice

Combine tomatoes and green chilies with water in a medium saucepan. Add bouillon cubes. Bring to a boil. Stir in seasonings and rice. Cover and let stand for 5 minutes.

Renae Gromatzky
Typist, Harris Farms Publishing

GREEN RICE

2 cups cooked rice
1 cup grated sharp Cheddar cheese
1/4 cup melted butter
salt & pepper
2 teaspoons chopped onion
1 cup chopped parsley
3 beaten egg yolks
3 stiff-beaten egg whites

Combine all ingredients except egg whites. Blend well. Fold in egg whites. Bake in greased dish at 350° for 25 minutes.

Sergeant George L. Turner, Company F, and wife Dana

DEVILED EGG CASSEROLE

6 hard-boiled eggs
1 teaspoon mustard
3 tablespoons sour cream
1 tablespoon finely chopped onion
1/4 teaspoon salt
1/2 cup chopped onion
1/3 cup chopped green pepper
1 can cream of mushroom soup
1 small jar pimientos
3/4 cup sour cream

Peel and halve eggs. Place yolks in small bowl and mash. Mix together mustard, 3 tablespoons sour cream, 1 tablespoon onion and salt. Pour over yolks and mix well. Stuff egg white halves and place in a casserole dish. Sauté 1/2 cup onion and green pepper. Mix well with soup, pimientos and 3/4 cup sour cream. Pour over eggs in casserole and bake at 350° until piping hot (about 20 minutes).

Bobby Poynter, Retired, and wife Jo

This recipe was given to us by Marietta Stark, wife of recently retired Drivers License Captain Robert A. Stark.

MOTHER'S NOODLES

- 1 cup sifted flour
- 1 teaspoon salt
- 2 beaten eggs
- 1 tablespoon milk

Sift flour and salt together. Add eggs and stir. Add enough flour to make a thick mixture. Add milk and work into the rest of the mixture. Dump out onto floured board and knead until enough flour is worked in to make a soft dough and you are able to roll it out without sticking. After rolling, dust with flour. Roll dough jelly roll fashion. Cut into thin strips, shake out and let dry. Cook in hot beef broth from Pot Roast.

Buzz Dulick, Texas Ranger Association Foundation, and wife Judy

SHERIFF'S HOT GARLIC CHEESE GRITS

- 1 cup uncooked grits
- 1 stick butter
- 1 (6 ounce) roll garlic cheese
- 1 (6 ounce) roll jalapeño cheese
- 6 ounces Cheddar cheese
- 1¼ cups milk
- dash hot pepper sauce
- dash of salt
- 5 eggs, slightly beaten
- paprika

Cook grits according to package directions. Add butter, cheese (chopped up), and milk. Set pan back on burner and stir until cheese melts. Add pepper sauce, salt and eggs. Turn into a buttered baking dish and sprinkle with paprika over the top. Bake at 350° for 45 minutes or until golden brown and set. Serves 8.

John Barron Harris, Texas Ranger Association Foundation, and wife Cheryl

GARLIC CHEESE GRITS

- **3¾ cups boiling water**
- **1 teaspoon salt**
- **1 cup instant grits**
- **½ cup margarine**
- **1 roll garlic cheese**
- **2 eggs**
- **milk**
- **1 dash hot pepper sauce**

Bring salted water to rolling boil. Slowly stir in grits. Cook 3 minutes, stirring constantly. Remove from heat and stir in margarine and cheese. Let stand until cheese is melted, stirring several times. Put eggs in cup and add enough milk to make 1 cup. Add egg mixture and pepper sauce. Bake in casserole at 300° for 1 hour.

Glenn Krueger, and wife Jackie

HOT DILL PICKLES

- **1 quart apple cider vinegar**
- **2 quarts water**
- **1 cup canning salt**
- **garlic**
- **fresh dill**
- **sliced onion**
- **jalapeño peppers**
- **small whole cucumbers**

Mix all ingredients together and bring to a boil. Pack quart jars with 1 pod of garlic, 1 sprig of fresh dill, ½ cup sliced onions and place ½ jalapeño pepper in the bottom. Pack in small whole cucumbers. Add ½ jalapeño pepper on top. Fill jars with the hot solution and then place sealed jars in a hot water bath for 10 to 15 minutes.

Bill Gunn, Retired,
and wife Sugar

This also works well with diced cucumbers.

LAURA'S CZECH PICKLES

Pack washed cucumbers tightly into quart jars. Add slice of onion, bud of garlic, large piece of fresh dill (stem & all), or 1 tablespoon of dried dill, ¼ teaspoon of turmeric, 1 jalapeño pepper and 2 tablespoons canning salt. Add ½ cup of vinegar and fill to within 1 inch of jar top with water. Heat in hot water bath until the cucumbers turn barely yellow. Remove and let cool. Do not over process.

James Wright, Retired,
and wife Laura

PICKLED PEPPERS & ONIONS

- jalapeño peppers
- 3 cups vinegar
- 3 cups water
- ⅓ cup salt
- 1 teaspoon olive oil
- sliced onion
- sliced carrots
- dash parsley flakes
- ½ teaspoon celery seed
- bay leaf
- slivered garlic

Split peppers, remove seed and pulp. Mix together seeds, pulp, vinegar, water, salt and oil. Bring to a boil. Strain and pour the liquid only over the pepper halves and let sit covered for 15 minutes. If you want a hotter pepper, leave the peppers whole and pour the liquid over the whole pepper. Take peppers out of liquid and pack into sterilized jars. To each jar add peeled sliced onions, carrot slivers, a dash of parsley flakes, ½ tablespoon celery seed, a bay leaf and garlic. Return liquid to boiling and pour over the peppers in the jar and seal.

Sergeant John Aycock,
Company F,
and wife Estelle

Don't get these near the horse at all!

PICKLED BEETS

- beets
- 1 quart 5% pickling vinegar
- 7 cups sugar
- 2 teaspoons pickling spice

Cut tops off beets and boil until done like potatoes. (About 1 hour in one cup of water.) Pour water off and dump beets in cold water. Slip off the skins and slice. Tie pickling spices in bag. Mix together vinegar, sugar and spices. Bring to boil. Put beets in solution and bring back to boil. Turn heat off as soon as it boils. Pack beets in quart jars that have been sterilized. Cover beets in solution. Seal with lids. Don't pack the jars in saddle bags. They will break and stick the leather together.

Sergeant John Aycock,
Company F,
and wife Estelle

RUBY RED CUCUMBER RINGS

- 2 gallons large cucumbers, sliced with seeds removed
- 2 cups hydrated lime
- 8½ quarts water
- 1 cup vinegar
- 1 tablespoon alum
- 1-2 bottles red food coloring
- 2 cups vinegar
- 2 cups water
- 10 cups sugar
- 8 cinnamon sticks
- 2 (8 ounce) packages red hot candy

Combine lime and 8½ quarts water. Put in cucumber rings and let stand for 24 hours. Drain. Wash in cool water, drain. Soak in cold water for 3 hours. (You can use ice cubes to get water quite cold.) Drain. Place 1 cup vinegar, alum and red food coloring in a large pot. Add cucumbers. Cover with water and heat to simmering. Cook for 2 hours. Drain. Combine 2 cups vinegar, 2 cups water, sugar, cinnamon sticks and red hots. Bring to a boil and pour over cucumbers. Let stand overnight. Repeat for 3 days. On the 4th day heat the solution and cucumbers. Pack in sterilized canning jars. Process in hot water bath.

Cathy Brumbalow
Office Manager,
Harris Farms

VALUABLE FACTS OR OLD WIVES TALES?

A small amount of cayenne pepper put into the water will somewhat neutralize the odor from boiling cabbage, cauliflower, onions, etc.

Cook green vegetables in water that is just beginning to boil and is slightly salted.

To beat egg whites quickly add a pinch of salt.

Dip hands in cold water before making pastry.

Sift baking powder with flour while dry.

Before using new cast iron pots, Dutch ovens, etc. boil potato peelings for one hour, then dry and rub with lard (shortening). Bake at 475° for 30 minutes. Turn oven off and allow to cool inside closed oven.

Tenderize tough meat by soaking in vinegar water for a little while.

Don't over-mix biscuits, it makes them tough.

Salad is better when torn by hand and served in a wooden bowl which has been rubbed with garlic. Hit lettuce on the stem end to remove core easily. I learned this when I first went into the hamburger business years ago.

Start vegetables in cold water if they grow under the ground and in boiling water if they grow above the ground (peas, greens, etc.). This was told to me years ago by Evelyn Price who was raised in Weatherford, Texas where lots of good vegetables grow.

Buy small or medium eggs. They're more nutritional than large eggs because they are laid by younger hens. This was told to me by Dean Stahman, Sr. who at that time was the largest egg producer in New Mexico. When we ate breakfast Mr. Stahman ate his eggs sunny side up because he said overcooking eggs destroyed some of the nutrients.

A few drops of vinegar added to boiling water in which an egg is to be poached will prevent the egg from breaking.

Boiled eggs will peel better when cracked and put in cold water after boiling.

Let chicken cool in broth before de-boning to have more flavor.

CONTRIBUTORS LIST

Norman Autrey, Retired
Sgt. John Aycock, Co. F & Wife Estelle
H. R. "Lefty" Block, Retired
Cathy Brumbalow
Tom Burks, Curator
Capt. Bruce M. Casteel, Headquarters Co.
Sgt. Barry K. Caver, Co. A
Sgt. Matt Cawthon, Co. F
C. J. "Buster" Collins, Co. E
Bob Connell, Retired & Wife Etta
Billy Crawford, Director of Texas Ranger Association Foundation
Sgt. Fred Cummings, Co. F & Wife Connie
Toliver H. Dawson, Retired
Capt. Jack Dean, Co. D & Wife Janie
Sgt. Kyle Dean, Co. B
John Dendy, Retired & Wife Vineta
Selwyn H. Denson, Retired & Wife Lois
Buzz Dulick, Texas Ranger Association Foundation & Wife Judy
Glenn Elliott, Retired
Lt. Robert C. Favor, Retired
Sgt. Brantley Foster, Co. B
Marie Garcia
Roberto D. Garza, Jr., Co. D
Sgt. W. R. "Bill" Gerth, Co. C & Wife Dixie
Sgt. Jim Gillespie, Co. C
Edgar D. Gooding, Retired
Tommy de Graffenried
Renae Gromatzky
Bill Gunn, Retired & Wife Sugar
Sgt. Jimmy T. Haile, Co. A
Sgt. Joe W. Haralson, Co. A
John Barron Harris, Texas Ranger Association Foundation & Wife Cheryl
Sgt. Gary S. Henderson, Co. F & Wife Sally
Sgt. H. Joaquin Jackson, Co. E
Lloyd Johnson, Retired
Glenn Krueger & Wife Jackie
Sgt. Johnny Krumnow, Retired
Weldon Lucas, Retired
John P. Lynch, Retired & Wife Dorothy
Ramiro "Ray" Martinez, Retired
Clayton McKinney, Retired
Sid Merchant, Retired
Sgt. James L. Miller, Co. F
Sgt. Morgan L. Miller, Co. D & Wife Ann
Capt. Bob Mitchell, Retired & Wife Jerry
Sgt. Donald R. Morris, Co. A & Wife Phyllis
Bill Nelson, Retired & Wife Joyce
Capt. Dan North, Retired & Wife Nancy
Sgt. Ray Nutt, Co. F
Jim Peters, Retired & Wife Lydia
Bobby Poynter, Retired & Wife Jo
Sgt. Jesse Priest, Retired
Bob Prince, Retired
Sgt. Tommy Ratliff, Headquarters Co.
Sgt. Danny Rhea, Co. B & Wife Sue
Texas Governor Ann W. Richards
Lewis C. Rigler, Retired
James L. Rogers, Retired
Phil Ryan, Retired
Charles Schreiner, III & Wife Karol
Sgt. Coy L. Smith & Wife Pat
Opal Smith
Wilson E. Speir & Wife Ann Marie
Wallace Spillar, Retired & Wife Ann
Sgt. George L. Turner, Co. F & Wife Dana
Jack Van Cleve, Retired & Wife LaVane
Capt. W. D. Vickers, Co. A & Wife Judy
John Vickery, Texas Ranger Association Foundation & Wife Patricia
Sgt. L. R. "Rocky" Wardlow, Headquarters Co.
Capt. Carl A. Weathers, Co. C & Wife Mickey
Capt. Walter A. "Bob" Werner, Retired & Wife Jeanne
Rhoda Willeford
Sgt. L. C. Wilson, Co. A
Max Womack, Retired
James Wright, Retired & Wife Laura
Sgt. Milton Wright, Co. A & Wife Marian
W. B. "Bill" Wright, Former Ranger

INDEX

To Order **The Authorized Texas Rangers Cookbook:**
Harris Farms Publishing
P.O. Box 191
Hamilton, Texas 76531

Please send me ______ copies @ $19.95 (U.S.) each $__________
Plus postage/handling @ $6.00 for one book $__________
and $1.00 for each additional book $__________
Texas residents add sales tax @ $1.60 each $__________
Enclosed is my check or money order in the amount of $__________

Name____
Address____
City______________________State__________Zip__________
Phone (day)____________________ (night)________________

— — — — — — — — — — — — — — — —

To Order **The Authorized Texas Rangers Cookbook:**
Harris Farms Publishing
P.O. Box 191
Hamilton, Texas 76531

Please send me ______ copies @ $19.95 (U.S.) each $__________
Plus postage/handling @ $6.00 for one book $__________
and $1.00 for each additional book $__________
Texas residents add sales tax @ $1.60 each $__________
Enclosed is my check or money order in the amount of $__________

Name____
Address____
City______________________State__________Zip__________
Phone (day)____________________ (night)________________

— — — — — — — — — — — — — — — —

To Order **The Authorized Texas Rangers Cookbook:**
Harris Farms Publishing
P.O. Box 191
Hamilton, Texas 76531

Please send me ______ copies @ $19.95 (U.S.) each $__________
Plus postage/handling @ $6.00 for one book $__________
and $1.00 for each additional book $__________
Texas residents add sales tax @ $1.60 each $__________
Enclosed is my check or money order in the amount of $__________

Name____
Address____
City______________________State__________Zip__________
Phone (day)____________________ (night)________________